SELF
STEERING

SELF STEERING

by

TOM HERBERT
25, Oakwood Gardens, Seven Kings, Essex, England.
FRITS FENGER
Rumgagger Farm, Norwell, Massachusetts, U.S.A.
STANLEY BRADFIELD
J. J. HERBULOT
MARCEL GIANOLI
Various A.Y.R.S. members and others.

EDITED BY
JOHN MORWOOD.

DIAGRAMS AND DRAWINGS BY
TOM HERBERT
JOHN MORWOOD
FRITS FENGER
NORMAN PEARCE
DAVID MOLE

3

THE AMATEUR YACHT RESEARCH SOCIETY

WOODACRES, HYTHE, KENT, ENGLAND.

This little book will be the first contact many people will have with the A.Y.R.S. so we feel it appropriate to say something about us. Our main objective is " to study everything about yachts, whether propelled by wind, power or human agency." We do this partly by instrumentation which has been invented by two of our *AMATEUR* members which can record the performance of full sized yachts from dinghies to twelve meters. It is perhaps noteworthy that no *PROFESSIONAL* firm has ever considered it worth its while to do this.

But the most exciting thing about us is our " avant garde " position in the yachting scene. We have, as members throughout the world, yachtsman who can think *originally*, and others who can develop these ideas in *practical terms*, as well as many others who are simply sympathetic to our work.

If you would like to learn more about your boat or do experiments or, still more, if you want to sail exciting boats at exciting speeds (possibly to exciting far away places) you may well find that the A.Y.R.S. is what you have been looking for.

In the past, many a lone sailor has tried to experiment with unusual craft, only to come across a barrier between himself and his fellow yachtsmen. These yachtsmen may have found it hard to understand what he was trying to do, or simply didn't want to know. We in the A.Y.R.S. unite all these experimenters, throughout the world, so that their ideas may be used for the improvement of all types of yachting.

If you had joined the A.Y.R.S. in 1955, you would have learned for the first time in all probability what a catamaran was. You would have found out that Indonesians had been sailing outriggers with floats on both sides for thousands of years while the Micronesians sailed their boats with either end as the bow. You would have found out that it was possible to stabilise a narrow hull with hydrofoils and learned that it was possible to sail off the water on hydrofoils.

Slowly, over the years, we have watched and studied the development of these exciting boats. Each year, we have given accounts of the catamarans which have appeared, noting their good points and making suggestions for their improvement. We have done the same with the double outrigger, now called the trimaran, writing up the work of the " lonely experimenters " till thousands are sailing.

This year (1966) may well be the " year of the flying sailing hydrofoil " because, thanks to the advice and design principles we have worked out, what looks like a fully controllable and safe flying sailing hydrofoil has appeared, costing little in money but capable of sailing at 24 knots in a 12 knot wind.

This book is a typical example of our work. The first edition appeared in 1957, when the " lonely experimenters " with their vane gears had only appeared in their ones and twos. Now, self steering gears are found all over the world and this book has become the standard work on the subject.

If you are interested in joining us, the subscription is small and the pleasure great. You will not just find out what yachting is now but what it is going to be in ten years' time. There are no qualifications for membership. Just write to the address shown on page 2.

EDITORIAL

January 1967 edition.

This publication was first produced in June, 1957. It was expanded in June, 1963, with the further information which had then come in. For this edition, however, it has all been carefully thought over and edited to give the most accurate and comprehensive picture available to date.

Tom Herbert, who was given the A.Y.R.S. file of correspondence by Peter Johnson in 1956, wrote and assembled our original publication. Tom collected the letters of A.Y.R.S. members and did a good deal of private research, producing an outstanding contribution to the subject. His deep insight into the subject has allowed him to invent the very astute gear which is shown later which may well be the best possible answer to the subject.

We are indebted to many people for the material in this publication. Firstly, to Tom Herbert and Peter Johnson. Then to the many inventors of the gears and methods of sheeting sails devised over the years. The celebrated French yachtsman, J. J. Herbulot, wrote a fine article in *BATEAUX*, extending our original study, while the tremendous contribution of Frits Fenger in designing twin running sails, one or both of which can give self steering on all courses, especially with his " Wishbone Rig " is of exceptional interest. We use his article " The Weather Twin " by courtesy of *RUDDER* magazine. We use the letter from the 1921 copy of *YACHTING MONTHLY* by kind permission of the Editor.

We are also indebted to Jock Burrough, John Hogg, André Kanssen and David Mole for reading the manuscript and making valuable suggestions.

INTRODUCTION.

SELF STEERING may be defined as the ability of a sailing boat to stay on a set course relative to the " apparent wind ". Only by the use of mechanical or electrical power can a boat be made to stay on a compass course with the possible exception of the wind-driven or water-driven gyroscopic gear which has so far remained undeveloped. It will be described later. All the rest of this publication will therefore deal with keeping a boat at a fixed angle to the apparent wind. Mechanical and electrical methods are too complex for us to study here and, in general, they have all been brought to near perfection by commercial interests.

Neither in speed or direction is the " apparent wind " the same as the " true wind " which blows over the water. The forward speed of the boat causes the " apparent wind " to blow more from the bow than the " true wind " and to increase its speed when close-hauled and reaching, decreasing the windspeed when running free.

The main function of the helmsman of a boat sailing close-hauled is to steer the boat so that he gets the highest speed to windward (the best Vmg) and generally this means that he stays at a set angle to the apparent wind. On other courses, a compass course may be steered. The main function of this book is to describe the techniques used to eliminate the need for a helmsman. On their own, these techniques do not enable a boat to sail accurately and safely from A to B. All they do is to relieve the crew of the continual and fatiguing job of keeping the boat moving fast in the right direction. The boat has still to be navigated and watches kept.

In narrow waters, hand steering is necessary or must be instantly available but in coastal cruising, steering can become the most disagreeable thing about sailing so self steering becomes desirable while, for ocean passages, particularly when single-handed, self steering has now become almost a necessity.

English yachting has been likened to a man sitting on a hard bench having buckets of cold water continuously thrown over him, whilst he tears up five pound notes. A good self steering device will enable him to tear up only a few more notes, but in reasonable comfort !

The Advantages of Self Steering

1. Sailing Efficiency. As soon as anything new appears, it is immediately criticised by the traditionalist. You hear self steering being referred to as " ugly " or " It's not as good as a human helmsman " etc.

6

The fact is, however, that when a self steering vane gear (The "*QUARTERMASTER*") was tested by instruments, it was found that the gear steered a better course to windward than a good human helmsman. The graphs shown on Page 8 were taken by John Hogg and show the better following of the wind variations by the vane than the human. This was a good helmsman and the charts of a bad or tired helmsman would have been much more in favour of the vane.

On reaching and running courses, the self steering gears may not be as good as the fresh and good helmsman because he can steer a compass course and anticipate waves before they come but the vane will often be better than a tired or bad helmsman. If the gyroscopic gear can be developed, for use in place of the vane on reaching and running courses, this deficiency could be removed.

2. Reduction of Weight. A good self steering gear can reduce the crew needed for a voyage by at least one person who will use up his own weight in food and water in 20 days. The boat would thus be about 200 lbs. lighter for a 20-day cruise.

3. Safety at Sea. Crew fatigue will be reduced and more efficient watch keeping is possible. Reefing may be done single-handed, and a change of fore sails made without disturbing the watch below.

The Faults of Self Steering Gears

1. All self steering gears need a certain minimum wind force to work them so many will not work in light or ghosting conditions, especially if there is a lumpy sea.

2. Running in large waves, vanes may temporarily lose the wind, either because the sea surface produces a large eddy of wind or because the boat surfs down the face of a wave so fast that it exceeds the speed of the wind, which can often happen with multihulls.

3. Self steering gears can only react to changes in conditions *AFTER* they arrive at the boat whereas a human can see them before they arrive and take action, though the vane's vigilance often outweighs the helmsman's anticipation.

4. The course sailed is never straight but wobbles around the large eddies in the wind. However, the mean wind direction is very true indeed because it is decreed by the atmospheric " Isobars " so the course sailed can be relied upon for navigational purposes, until a real shift of the wind occurs.

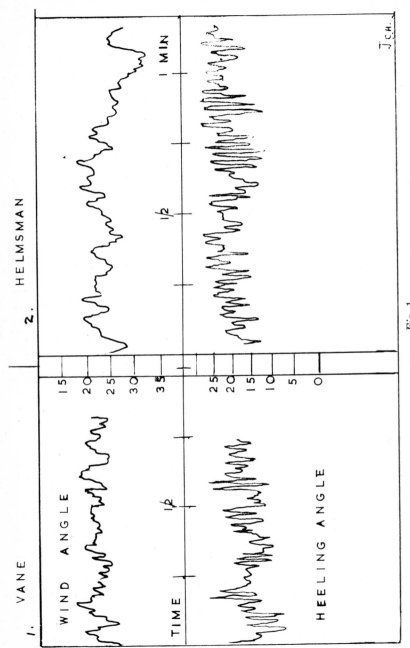

Fig. 1

VANE GEAR TEST

(A note on the measurement of a Vane-steered 5-ton Cruiser)

BY J. HOGG

Self steering gears have reached an interesting stage of development because they are now able to *sail* a yacht to windward rather than merely *steer* her on a general course. In other words the degree of control is sufficiently rapid and accurate to reduce the variations of the apparent wind angle to the minimum and to avoid oversteering. Comparative tests of a vane gear against a skilled helmsman, by means of the multipen chart recording equipment showed that the vane (a Quartermaster fitted to a 5-ton Cruiser) was sailing the yacht better than the helmsman, producing higher pointing, a lower average angle of heel and resulting in a better speed made good to windward. Although the vane could not anticipate the changes of wind flow, requiring action, the constant alertness and correct response of the vane offset this disadvantage and in comparison was more accurate than the helmsman who, although skilled was unable to concentrate to the extent that the vane could. Subsequently in sailing with others of similar class and size the vane steered yacht hauled out to windward by a remarkably large margin, which confirmed the results indicated by the tests with the recorder.

The figure shows typical extracts from recorder charts taken 1. with the Vane steering the yacht and 2. immediately afterwards with a skilled helmsman in control. The upper line in each case shows the variation of the ship's heading to the apparent wind. Ideally this should be as consistant as possible. In this case the helmsman is wandering slightly more than the vane gear and towards the right of the chart bears off quite appreciably due to a moments inattention, although being still quite close on the wind. He is not pointing as high, averaging 24° compared with the vane's 21° average in the period shown.

The lower lines show the heeling angles recorded at the same time, which change constantly as each wave hits the ship and also as the wind angles alter. Here again the Vane gear shows a better average heeling angle, 16° compared with the helmsman 24°, and since the speeds were similar this resulted in a lower leeway angle and a better speed made good to windward with the vane gear in control.

THE HISTORY OF SELF STEERING

Undoubtedly, various boats have been steered by their sails at various times since the beginning of sailing. The earliest boats were steered by paddles with little power and doubtless then, as now, these were sometimes lost or broken, leaving the boat uncontrollable, except by its sails. The paddles were converted into quarter rudders by the Ancient Egyptians. Doubtless in the larger craft, the loss of one of these would have been a matter of small moment. They often used several on each side and carried large crews of rowers. But the small inshore fisherman must, like many a yachtsman, have found his boat rudderless at one time or another and still have been able to sail back to port by manipulating his sails. He also probably learnt how to rig his boat so that he could leave the helm to attend to his fishing gear, thus producing self steering.

It is thus more than likely that every inshore fisherman from the beginning of time has known how to make his boat self steer or at least sail without a rudder and this probably explains the preference of all fishermen for at least two sails on their boats because it is impossible to make a boat self steer with only one sail and no rudder. With two sails, sheeting in the fore sail and letting out the aft one will cause the boat to bear away, while the reverse process will cause luffing.

The problem to the inshore fisherman was traditional and so was the cure, being handed down from father to son. It must also have been well known to deep water sailors because it is hardly conceivable that Joshua Slocum in 1895 would have set off on a voyage around the world on his own unless he believed that he could make *SPRAY* self steer while he slept. The only alternative would have been to heave-to every night and that would have prolonged his voyage to an impossible extent. Slocum was, of course, a professional sailor accustomed to all types of ship and rig, and had been owner and master of some. Living, as he did all his life amongst sailing boats and ships, and also reading widely, his fertile brain must have given the matter a lot of thought. Combined with this was the fact that there were, at that time, various men on the East Coast of America who had sailed across the Atlantic on their own, notably Howard Blackburn, both of whose hands had been lost by frostbite in his youth when the dory in which he was fishing off the Grand Banks of Newfoundland became separated from the parent ship in the depth of winter.

There was thus a good deal of expertise in self steering when Joshua Slocum set off on his epic voyage. Sloop rigged boats, if they have a long straight keel like Slocum's *SPRAY* can be made to self steer close hauled by sheeting in the jib a little more than is desirable for maximum efficiency and giving the mainsheet a few more inches of freedom than when sailing at their best. Then, finding a position of the tiller by trial and error and fixing it there, the boat will stay on course. This was the method undoubtedly used by both Blackburn and Slocum.

For the free running course, self steering is also possible but it requires the jib to be sheeted flat amidships so that it acts more like a wind vane, pulling the head of the boat off the wind. With the mainsheet let well out, however, there is a powerful luffing force from the mainsail which cannot be neutralised by fixing the tiller to windward because in a lull in the wind, the boat would gybe. It was probably to reduce this force that Slocum shortened the main boom of *SPRAY* before he started to cross the Pacific and made a mizzen to balance the boat close hauled and give the extra area. Even the conversion of *SPRAY* to a ketch, however, did not appear to satisfy the down-wind self steering requirement and at Samoa, Slocum took on a long bamboo pole which he set as a flying bowsprit, on the end of which he set his flat-sheeted jib. He at last had perfected his downwind rig and ran 2,700 miles from Thursday Island to Cocos Keeling Island with this. He says : " During these 23 days, I had not spent more than 3 hours at the helm, including the time occupied beating into Keeling Harbour. I just lashed the helm and let her go ; whether the wind was abeam or dead aft, it was all the same. She always sailed her course." The steering jib kept the bow pointing downwind; he could use his ordinary foresail and main as pulling sails, while his mizzen was furled.

Slocum was thus able to make *SPRAY* self-steer both close hauled and with the wind nearly dead astern. It is more than likely that he made her self-steer with the wind abeam by slackening off the sheet of the steering job. Alas, however, we have little modern evidence on this or any other of Joshua Slocum's methods, though copies of *SPRAY* have been built in recent times. It would be an interesting and possibly profitable field of research.

THE DYNAMICS OF SELF STEERING

The first requirement for self steering is a " balanced " boat—a boat which does not have a strong tendency to luff when she heels. Slocum's *SPRAY* was of this type. The large square-riggers had to be of this type ; otherwise their rudders could not have controlled them. Many modern yachts are completely balanced and can roll down to the gunwale with finger-light control on the tiller. But there is a school of thought which believes that a slightly unbalanced boat, which increases its weather helm when it heels, is slightly faster. However, for some yachts at least, this may only mean that the 3° or 4° of weather helm which so much improves the lateral resistance of a deep keeled yacht should be preserved when the boat heels and this needs greater force at higher speeds. No matter the cause, however, the imbalance would make self steering more difficult.

11

The second thing which makes self steering easier is to have a rig of sails which does not produce violent luffing moments when the sheet or sheets are eased. For instance, the American *CAT BOAT* with a single gaff sail set on a mast in the bows would be almost impossible to make self steer because of the terrific weather helm needed when the sheets are eased. The high aspect ratio Bermudian rig, with sail changes being made by setting larger or smaller foresails rather than by reefing the mainsail mostly keeps its centres in the same fore and aft position. It is thus a much easier rig to make self-steering than the old fashioned gaff rig, while perhaps the ketch, especially Frits Fenger's *WISHBONE KETCH*, (A.Y.R.S. No. 11) is the easiest of all to make self steer.

Rig Directional Stability. This is the name given by Tom Herbert to the capacity of a boat to remain on a fixed heading in respect of the wind by reason of the sails alone. It seldom if ever exists with any boat or ship whose sails are set to give the greatest speed but, if the foresail is pulled in more than it should be for the course concerned and the mainsail is farther out than is proper, " Rig directional stability" can be made to appear, and with it, self steering. We will run across this concept many times in this publication. We have already seen how Slocum used it to get self steering with *SPRAY*. The hove-to state with the foresail aback while the main is just drawing is an extreme state of it. Twin spinnakers set with their tacks near the mast and their clews well forward also belong to this concept, while the most stable weathercocking vane consists of two boards at an angle to each other with the apex pointing into the wind, as used in Marin Marie's gear on *ARIELLE*.

THE MODEL YACHTSMEN

Most yachtsmen are Walter Mittys, the celebrated character whose day dreams were realities to him. When the quiet living man steps into his dinghy, he becomes a Columbus, Magellan, Drake or Slocum, while quite a few when racing, obviously become Captain Blights to judge from their language and treatment of their crews. What yachtsmen so often want to do is, I feel, to live the part of their " character " and to do that, they must sail a boat and this boat can be an ocean racer, cruiser, day boat or dinghy. Or, it can be a model yacht.

Now, late last century the sport of model yachting grew up. It may well have taken its origin from old Nat Herreshoff in the U.S.A. who encouraged it, and used to sail models of his full sized designs, though the English model yachting was at least as extensively practised as the American, one of the remarkable sights of London, to the foreigner, being elderly gentlemen running around the Round Pond after their model boats.

Probably, the origins of model yachting are lost in obscurity as men have always modelled their boats and ships and must often have sailed them. Certainly, the Malays and Micronesians were racing models when first visited by Europeans so that they must have had some self steering method. But what has characterised the modern model yachtsman more than anything else is his pre-occupation with gears and devices to steer his craft.

Mizzen of Thames Barge sheeted to tiller extension

The exact development of model yacht gears is not known at present but it is believed that the first device to enable models to steer themselves on reaching and running courses was a simple extension of the tiller aft of the rudder stock and taking one part of the sheet to this as used in the little mizzen of the Thames barge, though this sail also helps putting about. The idea of this was that, when the wind blew stronger and the boat heeled, more weather helm was needed to counteract the griping of the unbalanced hulls of the time. However, it was soon found that the device was improved by an elastic centering device to remove the weather helm quickly when the weight of wind left the sails as shown on Page 16. Another variation of the same theme was to put a weight on the aft extension of the tiller and again, heeling would give extra weather helm. This gear would also have needed some centering elastic but it never seems to have been much used.

The gear just described held a place in model yacht steering for some time but had the fault that, if the sails were caught aback, the boat would put herself on the opposite tack and stay there so the Braine gear was invented which, by suitably arranging the sheets on a quadrant would restore the boat to the original tack. This was a distinct improvement on the simple sheet to aft-pointing tiller and held the field for many years.

The final stage of model yacht self steering took place largely after 1930 when very high aspect ratio mainsails and jibs came into vogue. The art of yacht design had by then advanced to the stage where it was possible to design a yacht which was very easy to steer whether heeled or upright, largely through the theories of Admiral Turner and Harrison Butler—the so-called " Metacentric shelf theory." The theory may be erroneous but the yachts it produced were certainly well balanced. The model men took these theories to their hearts and soon started to make some lovely models which sailed well and needed very little help from self steering gears of any kind. This then made it possible for wind vane steering to be used, the only mechanism needed being some type of gear to change the direction of rotation between the vane and the rudder. This was firstly done by intermeshing cog wheels as in the Ballantyne gear but the mechanical advantage between the vane and the rudder cannot be altered. The modern practice is therefore to use the Fisher gear which consists of two slotted bars. one attached to the vane pivot and the other to the rudder stock. A small bolt is put through both slots but it can be attached to one of them while the other can rotate around it. The advantage of the Fisher gear is that the mechanical advantage between the vane and the rudder can be easily varied to give more steering power on a running course, when the relative wind is light and less steering power on a close-hauled course, when the relative wind is strong. This gear is shown as used by Mike Henderson's *MICK THE MILLER* on page 41.

THE CLASSIFICATION OF SELF STEERING GEARS

Self steering gears fall into four rough headings as follows :—
1. " Sheet to tiller " gears.
2. Vane gears working directly on the rudder.
3. Vane gears which use the wind or waterflow to work the rudder.
4. Gyroscopic gears.

14

Sheet to Tiller Gears. These include :

a. The aft-pointing tiller.
b. The Braine gear.
c. The Weather-pulling sheet where an end of the mainsheet is attached to the tiller through a block on the *Weather* gunwale, pulling against shock cord to lee.
d. The Lee-pulling sheet (Johnson gear) where an end of the main-sheet is attached to the tiller through a block on the *Lee* gunwale, pulling against shock cord to weather.
e. Twin spinnakers.
f. Twin foresails.
g. The " Weather twin " as devised by Frits Fenger.
h. The boomed jib on the permanent backstay.

Vane Gears. In all these, it helps if the rudder is " balanced " to avoid excessive vane size. We say a rudder is balanced if part is before the axis of rotation and this part should not exceed one-sixth of the total area or the rudder may not align with the water flow.

a. The Ballantyne gear.
b. The " Rotating Carriage " gear, which gives continuous and easy course setting.
c. The Fisher gear (slotted rods)
d. The running line gears of Mike Henderson.

Wind and Water Flow Gears.
a. The Windmill gear.
b. The horizontally pivoted vane gear.
c. The trim-tab on rudder gears.
d. The Hasler Pendulum-Servo gear (athwartships swinging servo blade.)

Wind Driven Gyroscopic Gears.
a. The gyroscope in place of the vane.
b. The *PEN DUICK II* gear.

SHEET TO TILLER GEARS

These gears use the variations in wind pressure on the sails to control the rudder and were developed for models in the days when the gaff rig was used and the hulls had a tendency to turn into the wind when the pressure on the sails increased, due to the alteration of the immersed shape of the hull on heeling and, on free courses, the griping force of the low aspect ratio mainsail with long boom.

15

The performance of a sheet to tiller gear when close hauled or reaching is quite good with the hull and rig for which it was developed because it neutralises the griping, while the sails can be trimmed to have " Rig directional stability ". But, as the sheets are freed, the sails can no longer be made to self steer and the gear becomes more difficult to adjust and less reliable. In fact, on a broad reach, or a run, the sail plan has to be adjusted with more sail area forward in order to make the boat keep on course. The modern model yacht is well balanced and does not gripe on heeling as much as those of a generation ago so these gears have gone out of fashion with model yachtsmen but they can be of great value in full sized yachts, either on their own or as an addition to a vane gear.

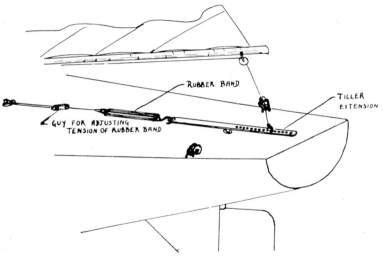

Fig. 2. A Model " Sheet and Tiller " Gear

The Aft-Pointing Tiller. Fig. 2 shows the set-up for the model yacht. The mainsheet is hooked somewhere along the aft extension of the tiller in a position to give the pressure on the helm needed to keep the boat on course. The centering elastic or shock cord is then adjusted in pull to overcome the inherent friction of the gear and return the rudder amidships if the wind pressure on the sails decreases.

Schuyler Seward has experimented with this type of gear on the 30 ft. ketch *WILD SURMISE.* He led the mizzen sheet through a block on the tiller extension which was adjusted in length until the boat settled down on course. No centering shock cord was used and the gear steered the boat satisfactorily for three hours until the makeshift tiller extension carried away.

The Braine Gear. This is a modification of the previous gear so that, if a model should tack itself, it will automatically go back to the original tack. Or, by suitably adjusting the variables, the model will sail equally well on both tacks. With this gear, two mainsheets are used, each of which passes through a block on its own side of the yacht and then crosses over to the opposite side where it is hooked onto a quadrant on the rudder head as shown in Fig. 3. The quadrant has a number of holes drilled in it (in a separate arc for each mainsheet) so that the power exerted by the sheet on the rudder may be altered. The two mainsheets join near the boom and the combined sheet passes through a block about half way along the boom, then to another block at the aft end of the boom and, from there, it goes to the aft deck where it can be adjusted for various courses.

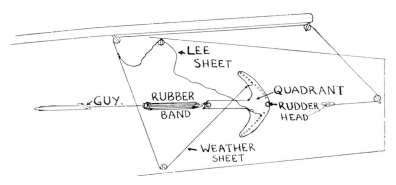

Fig. 3. Braine Gear

In operation, the lee sheet is always slack while the weather sheet controls the rudder, giving it weather helm from the lee arm of the quadrant.

The Braine gear can be used on full sized boats and its facility of automatic tacking can be used as long as there is a self-acting jib. By hooking the slack sheet nearer to the rudder head than the other one, the boat will automatically return to the correct tack, if she should be put about either by a windshift or a wave.

Apart from the automatic tacking, the only advantage of the Braine gear over the ordinary sheet to tiller gears which will be described later is that the quadrant enables it to be adjusted without

17

disturbing the trim of the sails. The performance is similar and it appears to work best when coupled to a broad shallow rudder.

Sopranio's Gear. SOPRANINO, a 20 foot sloop, used a simplified form of the Braine gear on her Atlantic crossing with Pat Ellam and Colin Moodie in 1951. This is shown in Fig. 4. The rearward facing quadrant is fitted with a length of mast track and the mainsheet is led from a central block on the counter forward under the horse to a locking sail slide on the quadrant. The sail slide is moved round the quadrant to the weather side of the boat until she

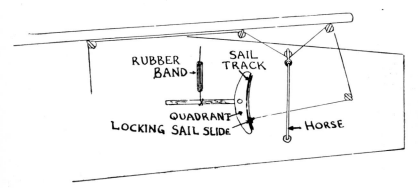

Fig. 4. *Sopranino's Braine gear*

settles down on course, an elastic band being used to bias the helm as required. Schuyler Seaward, who now owns *SOPRANINO*, writes of this gear : " It works poorly with a breeze on the quarter but improves the closer you sail to a beat. I have spent two days without touching it when single-handed, mostly below brewing up and eating goodies."

The Weather Pulling Sheet. Tiller extensions and quadrants seem to frighten many people. Fortunately for them, the same results can be got by leading the sheet through a block on the weather gunwale and then to the tiller as in Fig. 5. The centering shock cord may be led forward or to the lee gunwale as desired. To work properly, this system must have the minimum of friction in both the block and rudder pintles. It is, however, desirable to limit the amount of weather helm produced either by pins in a rail or a lanyard from the lee gunwale.

The Lee Pulling Sheet (Johnson Gear). Peter Johnson (the original A.Y.R.S. " Correspondent on self steering " worked out a sheet to tiller gear for his yacht which is shown in Fig. 6. This

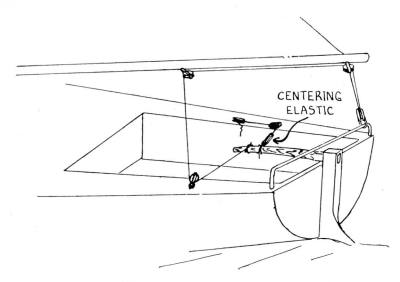

Fig. 5.   Sheet to tiller gear

method looks very similar to the previous one but it is very different in function. As opposed to the previous method, the mainsheet pulls the tiller to *Lee*, not to weather, but it is again balanced by shock cord.   The effect of this is that the whole mainsail is made to act like a vane and, on a reaching course, for example, if the wind comes freer, the mainsail makes the boat luff or alternatively, if the wind comes more from the bow, the shock cord pulls the tiller to weather.

Comparison between Weather and Lee Pulling Sheets. We feel that, with a well balanced boat close-hauled or close reaching, the lee pulling sheet would be a more reliable method than the weather pulling sheet but it cannot be used with the wind much aft of the beam when the weather pulling sheet can still be used.   However, as the same gear is used for both, a change-over will present no difficulty.

The Boomed Backstay Jib. When a yacht has a permanent backstay, a jib can have a club fitted at its foot and be hoisted up it.   The sheet on the club can be double and led through blocks on the quarters and then to the tiller.   This arrangement would then function as a large vane gear.   Because of the slope of the backstay, it might not work well with the wind before the beam but it should work well with the wind aft, though it would foul the boom on a gybe.

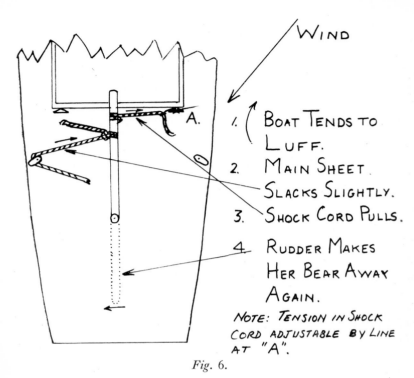

WIND

1. (BOAT TENDS TO
   LUFF.
2. MAIN SHEET
   SLACKS SLIGHTLY.
3. SHOCK CORD PULLS.

4. RUDDER MAKES
   HER BEAR AWAY
   AGAIN.

NOTE: TENSION IN SHOCK
CORD ADJUSTABLE BY LINE
AT "A".

Fig. 6.

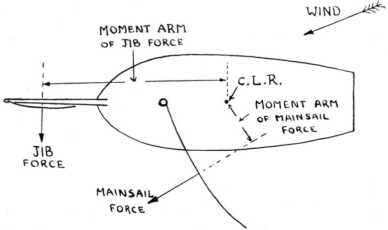

WIND

MOMENT ARM
OF JIB FORCE

C.L.R.

MOMENT ARM
OF MAINSAIL
FORCE

JIB
FORCE

MAINSAIL
FORCE

Fig. 7 " SPRAY " Self Steering Downward

20

Downwind Rigs

There are not many fore and afters who can self steer downwind. One of the notable exceptions was Slocum's *SPRAY*, which, as already mentioned, sailed downwind with the mainsheet eased right off and her " flying jib " sheeted hard in amidships with the helm lashed as necessary. Fig. 7 shows the set up. The line of action of the force acting on the mainsail forms a couple tending to make the boat rotate into the wind. The force acting on the jib also forms a couple but this is in opposition to the mainsail couple and it is presumed that the moments of these couples were equal and opposite so that balance was maintained. The rudder also forms a couple to help the jib balance the large mainsail force, if required.

Self Steering with a Squaresail

The squaresail, when used downwind, balances the boat but on its own does not give the boat directional stability. A steering gear is therefore necessary and the only type of gear which would be reliable with it is some type of vane gear. *BUTTERCUP* used a vane gear with her squaresail for her Atlantic crossing in 1956 and, from all reports, it functioned very well.

If a squaresail is braced in, the boat's balance is slightly upset because the line of action of the propulsive force forms a couple about the C.L.R. as shown in Fig. 8. However, by setting a jib from the main halyard with its tack led aft and the clew sheeted to the weather side, a couple is formed which will help to balance the boat and produce directional stability. If this jib is boomed and has two sheets led through blocks to the tiller, it will function as a type of vane gear and will also help to prevent the rhythmic rolling which tends to occur when sailing under the squaresail. If there is a permanent backstay, the jib can be hanked to it with the clew forward.

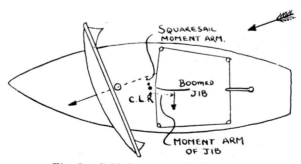

Fig. 8   Self Steering with Squaresail

21

Otway Waller

This rig was invented and first used by Captain Otway Waller in 1930 on his yawl *IMOGEN* in which he made a single-handed passage from Limerick in Ireland to Las Palmas in the Canaries. As shown

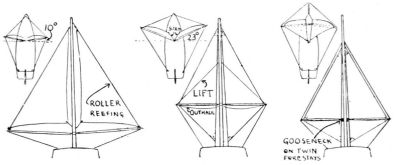

Fig. 9 *Otway Waller*   *Frederick A. Fenger*   *Marin-Marie*
" *Twin* " *Rigs*

in the drawing of Fig. 9, the rig consisted of two triangular sails with their peaks at the mast and the tacks at the ends of two spinnaker poles. Wykeham-Martin roller reefing gear was used so that either sail could be taken in by rolling it around its stay. The sails were sheeted to the mast and the poles were trimmed so that each was about 10° forward of athwartships. Lines from the ends of the poles ran to quarter blocks and from there to the tiller.

In use, when the yacht yawed at all from her course, the pressure on the weather sail increased and that on the lee sail decreased. These forces were then passed from the poles to the tiller which steered the boat back on course. Forward preventers were used in case of a sudden backwinding.

The Fenger Modification

In 1932, Frederic A. Fenger published the results of model experiments in *Yachting* in which he showed that by increasing the angle of dihedral from 10° to 23° and by spreading the two sails apart by some 3 to 4 feet on deck, the rig was directionally stable and no connection between the booms and tiller was necessary. In the Fenger modification, the luffs were brought to jackstays near the mast and the clews were sheeted to the ends of the poles, thus raising their height above the waves. Reefing could either be by Wykeham-Martin gear or by dropping the peaks.

The Marin-Marie Twins

With this rig which Marin-Marie independently invented and used on *WINIBELLE II* on a single-handed Atlantic crossing in 1933, there were two forestays set a little apart. On each of these stays, a sail was set which was sheeted to a pole at its outboard end. Like Waller's rig, lines ran from the ends of the poles through blocks to the tiller. Like the Fenger modification of Waller's rig, the clews were high up. The two sails of this rig had no dihedral; in fact there was anhedral but it still worked well and even allowed a large spinnaker to be set in light winds and the self steering still worked. The sails were taken in by dropping the peaks.

THE VALUE OF TWINS

These rigs are used on the long downwind runs which are possible in the trade wind areas. Their advantages over the squaresail with balancing jib are :

1. The gear is not so complicated.
2. It is less liable to chafe.
3. It is easier to keep the gear from fouling the standing rigging.

The disadvantages are that under twins, a boat is not very manoeuverable and it is not easy to make it self steer on any course other than a run dead downwind.

The twin rigs' sails are either called " Spinnakers " or " Staysails " but it is difficult to differentiate between them because they are all made of heavy canvas. By definition, a staysail is set on a stay and a spinnaker is set flying. On this basis, the staysails are easier to handle. The self steering properties depend more on the way the sails are set rather than on any particular merit in the sail itself. John Goodwin, who described his crossing from Gibraltar to Barbados in the *SPEEDWELL OF HONGKONG* in the October 1956 *Yachting Monthly* used both staysails and spinnakers, depending on the sail area required. Both appeared to work well.

When running dead downwind, the first essential of self steering, *Balance*, is achieved by setting two sails of equal area on either side of the boat. The second essential, *Directional Stability*, is achieved by setting them so that they present a dihedral angle to the wind. To augment this, the staysail sheets (or spinnaker guys) can be led back to the tiller, the twins acting like a crude vane. The staysail appears to be better than a spinnaker from the self steering point of view because it is cut flat and is less liable to collapse if the boat yaws violently off course.

23

On a course directly downwind, maximum directional stability is obtained by setting the twins from the stemhead of the boat as in Marin-Marie's twins. If the course is not directly downwind, however, this position has the disadvantage that the sails are too far forward and the boat's balance is upset. To restore balance and increase speed, a small jib set back to front abaft the mast helps when the wind is on the quarter. Alternatively, the rudder can be biassed with rubber bands, the amount of bias being adjusted until the boat settles down on course. John Goodwin used the stemhead position on *SPEEDWELL OF HONGKONG*, and biassed the helm when necessary with shock cord.

Commander Victor Clark describing the self steering arrangements on his 9 ton ketch *SOLACE* in the February 1956 *Yachting Monthly*, set his twin staysails on jackstays led to the foot of the mast as in the Fenger twins. To achieve a comparable " Rig Directional Stability " with the twins further aft, the dihedral angle of the sails needs to be greater, but the boat is easier to balance with the wind on the quarter. Commander Clark set his mizzen to improve speed and balance and biassed the self steering with an " Inhaul."

With most of the " Twin " rigs, reefing can be easily carried out by letting the booms swing forward to reduce the area presented to the wind. This increases the dihedral angle and hence the " Rig Directional Stability " which is useful because of the increased tendency to yaw due to the rougher sea conditions. In practice, however, this simple method of reefing is seldom done. It is more usual either to roll up the sails with a Wykeham-Martin gear or drop the peaks, should a trade wind squall need a reduction of canvas.

Many prominent yachtsmen have used and experimented with the " Twin Headsail " rig on Ocean voyages. All of those who have written of their cruises with it have contributed something to the design and use of the rig and, though we have given some account of it here, there is still a wealth of practical detail in their writings which cannot be included in this booklet.

THE FENGER GILL TWINS

Undoubtedly the greatest contribution to Ocean Cruising is the development of the twin rigs for running down the Trade winds. Invented by Captain Otway Waller, improved by Frederick A. Fenger and perfected by George Gill, they remove what Sidney Howard, who cruised from the Thames to Tahiti, called "The Tyranny of the Tiller." This rig has converted Ocean Cruising from hard work to pleasure.

Appraisal and study of the various twin rigs is within the scope of the A.Y.R.S. but it is thought better for this publication just to rely on the judgement of Frits Fenger and describe the Gill twins, as the ones to recommend for any would-be Ocean Cruiser. It is pointed out that Frits has studied twins in all their forms both in models and full scale, has done smoke flow tests and other tests as well and must have put in more hours of thought on them than any other person. The reason Frits prefers the Gill twins is because they are simple, safe and they work.

The Gear. This consists of 1. Two deck eyebolts. 2. Two tack pendants. 3. Halyards. 4. Spinnaker plates on the mast. 5. Two poles. 6. Guys and 7. The sails. The only attachments to the yacht are the two eyebolts and the plates on the mast. No jackstays or lifts are used.

The Main Features. The Gill twins are set flying from the deck eyebolts to the halyards. Their clews are held out by spinnaker poles and are cut high so that the poles come down clear of the rail and deck, bringing the clews with them, when the sail is lowered. By spacing the deck eyebolts a little from each other and setting the sails forward by 23°, as shown by Frits Fenger, the after guys need not be attached to the tiller, and the ship runs smoothly.

The Sail. This is a triangular sail cut to have a circular arch. The distance from the clew to the luff is 30% of the length of the luff and the clew should be the same distance above the tack. The maximum area for one man to work should not be more than 240 square feet.

The Eyebolts. Each tack eyebolt is placed away from the midline of the yacht by 3% to 4% of the height of the halyard block to the deck and it is about the same distance forward of the mast. The distance between the two eyebolts must be not less than 1 ft. 6 in. This position gives a gap between the luffs of the sails which clears the " Dead air " from behind them and gives a steadier inflow and increases the self steering qualities so that the after guys need not be attached to the tiller. Being forward of the mast gives some lift which is about 10% of the sail force but the main reason for this is to allow the poles to come down clear when the sail is lowered and to keep the sails away from them near the mast.

The Mast Plates. The mast plates and spinnaker poles may be of the usual pattern or they may be as in the accompanying drawing by Frederick Fenger. The mast plates should be placed on the forward quadrant of the mast so that the thrust force does not produce a wringing strain on the mast. The slotted tangs of the poles can easily be slipped over the $\frac{1}{2}$ in. pins in the toggles and they will not come out with ordinary use. The angle 15° of the slot will also keep the pole from coming adrift when hanging down the mast in a temporary stow.

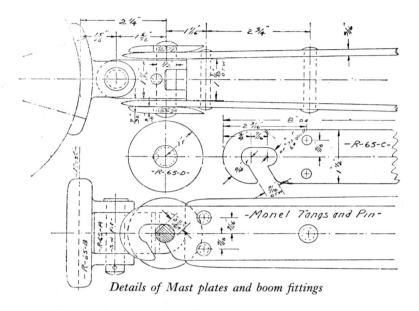

Details of Mast plates and boom fittings

The Spinnaker Poles. These should not be more than 16 feet long at the most for single handed work. The inboard end can have the attachment shown, the outboard end a fitting with three eyes or loops.

The Halyard. One may use 5/32 in - 7 x 19 stainless wire, rendering through a block having a suitable sheave $3\frac{1}{2}$ in. and hung about 3 ft. above the head of the sail from a strop around the mast. At the hauling end, there should be an open snatch block with a $\frac{3}{8}$ in. or $\frac{7}{8}$ in. manila tail spliced in its becket. The tack pendant may be of the same wire, with a snap shackle to the deck eyebolt.

Hoisting the Sail. The tack pendant is shackled on to the eyebolt giving a distance of about 1 ft. 6 in. from the tack to the deck. This will give good visibility when the sail is hoisted and clearance from a rolling sea. The clew of the sail is secured to the upper forward eye on the end fitting of the spinnaker boom, the fore guy to the lower forward eye and the after guy to the after eye. The fore guy is left slack and the aft guy is belayed abreast the cockpit with just enough

26

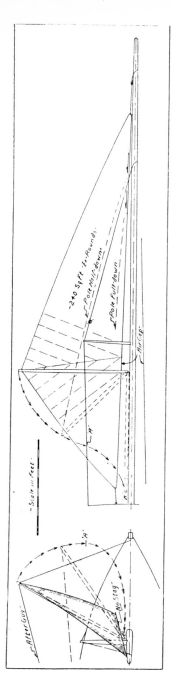

scope so that the pole can hang into the mast. The halliard is then attached to the peak and the sail hoisted. As the sail goes up, the pole goes forward and rises up in an arc to its proper position. When the running snatch block of the halyard comes to hand, the manila tail is cast under a snatch block on the mast about two feet above the deck, back into the running block on the halyard and one now has a three part purchase for setting up.

When the sail is up, the after guy is trimmed so that the spinnaker boom is 23° forward of athwartships, which is the angle found to give the best directional stability. It is most important to have a tight luff and the spinnaker pole of such a length that the clew is well pulled out. Also both fore and aft guys must be set up tight so as to anchor the clew firmly in position. A swaying sail produces a rolling boat and twins with well anchored corners steady the vessel.

Lowering the Sail. Neither guy is touched. The halyard is firstly eased away and the sail comes down, the spinnaker pole swinging forwards and down in an arc as shown in the diagram. It swings down over the rail and should come in sweetly just above the deck. It brings the clew with it and the sail should then be easy to manage with one hand while the rest of the sail is lowered.

References. Other articles on " Twins " by Frits Fenger are " *The Weather Twin—A steering Sail* " *Yachting*, December, 1953,

27

and "*Twin Spinnakers Versus Twin Staysails*" *The Rudder*, July, 1956. We are grateful to the Editors of these two magazines for permission to use the two drawings reproduced here.

SELF STEERING WITH THE WEATHER TWIN
BY Frederic A. Fenger

When first the weather twin was applied in my little *DIABLESSE*, no thought was given toward using it for self-steering. It was merely a replacement for the headsail—when the wind was brought on the quarter—and also, due to its weather position somewhat of a counter-balance against the rounding-to action of the after sails. The weather helm which, on this occasion, often has grown to a considerable extent, was appreciably reduced and this should have given me the hint toward ultimate self-steering with this sail. But I was quite content to leave my self-steering to the close-hauled courses—which

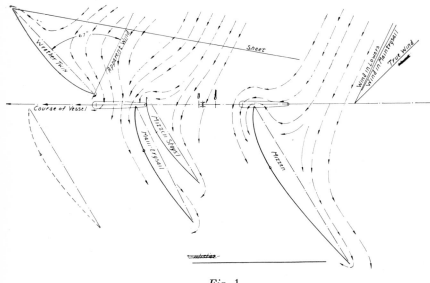

Fig. 1

can be irksome at times—and to sailing directly down wind under twin spinnakers. After all, why not sit back and tool the wheel at one's ease if the little ship is making gainful knots.

But with the increasing demand for self steering throughout the entire range from close-hauled to directly down-wind, on the part of lone Englishmen racing across the Atlantic and who have been using the cumbersome and generally complicated vane-rudder-tab-cum-

Fig. 2   *With the wind on the quarter, all plain sail can be carried together with the twin which does all the work*

topsail-spanker arrangements to keep their small vessels on approximate courses, it occurred to me that one might attain the same objective, yet to better effect, by a more fundamental approach via the weather twin, so trimming it that a reverse flow through the sail—from leech to luff—might entirely cancel out the rounding-to effect of the after sails and thus bring on a continual zero helm—or self steering. My concept hinged upon trimming the sail for maximum effectiveness at about twenty-three degrees on the either side of ninety degrees, so that the wind would impinge upon the cloth at about sixty-seven degrees. Then, as the vessel tended to round to, the after sails would begin to lose some of their drive while the weather twin, still pulling effectively, would ease the vessel back upon her course.

On the other hand, were the vessel to fall off, the weather twin would start to lose some of its leverage against the after sails which, in turn, largely have retained their lateral components so that they nudge the vessel up on her course again.

It was a pretty theory, yet worth looking into for I found some encouragement from the old ship masters who, in order to reduce yaw when sailing close-hauled, braced their yards less sharply on the mainmast than on the fore and, likewise, less sharply on the mizzen than on the main. Then a yaw, or sudden shift of wind, would bring the mizzen yards aback first, while the forward yards still were drawing. The resultant couple thus swings the vessel's head off and leaves her sailing on course.

After diagramming forces, I came to the conclusion that this weather twin with reverse flow was worth a try.

At the time, Stanley Bradfield, sailing from Australia under my main-trysail rig, had arrived in Aden where I wrote him at length, going into considerable detail with sketches, so that he might try out his weather twin for self steering.

To my surprise and delight, he replied that he had already sailed most of his trackage across the Indian Ocean while sheeting the weather twin exactly as I was suggesting and that he now had self steering whenever he wanted it, on all courses. Since he had made this first application—on his own initiative—I urged that he write the following article and thus establish *his* priority.

Illustration No. 1 shows my proposed sheetings, which had been anticipated by Bradfield. In illustration No. 2, Bradfield's *D'VARA* has the wind on her quarter but with the forestaysail still drawing. So much the better, when it is not blowing too hard ! In a recent conversation with a friend for whom I had made a weather twin application, I was told that when using the genoa in the lighter airs, his son had carried the twin tack forward, thus using the sail more as a weather staysail, so that the flow in the genoa had been augmented and the vessel's speed increased accordingly. In my own vessel, I have been trimming my main-trysail and mizzen staysail, both on the same side, for reverse flow, in order to promote better inter-action between the lowers when sailing directly down wind.

I shall not venture to predict how this method may work with a single-masted rig.

D'VARA'S sailing with "The Weather-Twin" by Stanley Bradfield.

In recent years there has been a spate of systems designed to allow small yachts to steer themselves in any weather and on any course allowed by the wind. Many ideas have been tried from mechanical and hydraulic systems, through wind vanes, to the direct utilization of the sails, and each of these methods has its proponents. The 1960 singlehanded race gave proof that wind vanes are entirely practicable and, of course, there are several automatic pilot systems which have given excellent service for many years. However, the most successful methods, to date, require special equipment, most of which is expensive, and they cannot be adapted to all sailing craft.

Our yacht, the thirty-foot canoe-sterned *D'VARA*, is to the design of Harrison Butler, but carries a main-trysail rig by Fenger. Under this rig she is easily controlled, handy, manoeuvres well and is so balanced that she will sail to windward with the tiller free.

The southwest monsoon was very light when we left Addu and for five days *D'VARA* headed southward with no one at the tiller, but then, after a short calm, a new wind came in from the northeast, making our best course a dead run. It was really too light for the twin spinnakers, so I decided to try out a system of self steering that I had been mulling over for months. After dropping the fore-staysail and booming out the main-trysail, mizzen staysail and mizzen to port, the starboard twin spinnaker was hoisted, the after guy, or sheet, being led through a quarter block and attached to the tiller. The pull of the sheet was counteracted by rubber shockcord which led from the tiller to the lee cockpit coaming.

At first it took some time to get the correct adjustment but when it was finally found, *D'VARA* headed off happily downwind and required no further help. Later the wind increased to force five, and for some time the yacht sailed by the lee, but before she got far enough around to gybe, the spinnaker lost the wind, thereby decreasing the pull on the sheet and allowing the tiller to be brought to leeward by the shockcord. Until the tension on the shockcord was increased, the yacht's course varied from dead before the wind to where the wind was approximately fifteen degrees on the leeward quarter, but, with the adjustments made, she again took up the set course and it was fascinating to watch the tiller doing its job with no outside help.

A couple of days later, the wind dropped, then came in from the southeast and we were able to head west towards our destination. The sails were gybed over, the port twin set, and off we went again, this time with the wind on our quarter. In fact, for the greater part of the time, the wind was from south-southeast resulting in the apparent wind going almost abeam, but it was only necessary to trim the sails, and adjust the tension of the shockcord to keep the yacht on course. At times the wind went up to force six and it became necessary to hand the main trysail, but this made no difference in the self steering ;

Self steering with the weather twin was first attempted on the passage between the Maldive and Seychelle islands. The gear was all makeshift, but functioned perfectly. Note the pins to limit the tiller's swing

evidently the increased turning moment of the mizzen compensated for the reduction in sail farther forward.

After fifteen days at sea, Frigate Island, easternmost sentinel of the Seychelles, lifted from the sea ahead and, during this time, I calculated that we had spent no more than twelve hours at the tiller. On the next passage, 1,500 miles to Aden, *D'VARA* again steered herself in winds of varying strength and direction averaging over 100 miles a day.

Experience on these two passages showed that it was advisable to limit the travel of the tiller in gusty conditions, so that corrections to the course were not too violent.   Fortunately there was a rack already mounted on the after cockpit coaming into which pins could be inserted to hold the tiller in any given position and, now, by spacing the pins at equal distance each side of the tiller, its travel could be controlled.   It was also possible to steer up to ten degrees either side of the base course by moving the weather or leeward pin and thereby restricting the movement of the tiller in that direction.

Later correspondence with Fenger revealed that I had hit upon a system which he had foreseen, but had not carried through to actual sailing trials.   He pointed out that, in theory, with the weather twin sheeted to sixty-seven degrees forward of the apparent wind, there was reverse flow across the sail; i.e., the wind flow was from leech to luff and, consequently, the weather twin could be sheeted much farther aft than when the flow was from luff to leech, as it usually is. (Also, this reverse flow speeds up the direct flow under the lee of the following working sail, and into the belly of the headsail or Genoa, when they are carried also.   F.A.F.).

When sailing with the twin sheeted in this position, a departure from the set course resulted in an immediate correction.   When the yacht headed up, the increased drive as the leech approached the luffing point augmented the pull on the sheet and the tiller was hauled to weather until the hull returned to her set course and the pull and counter-pull balanced once more. On the other hand, when the yacht veered to leeward of the course, the sail lost some of its drive and then the shockcord was able to overcome the pull of the sheet and so drag the tiller to leeward.   In practice, the yacht steered an extremely good course—in steady winds within two degrees of the set course, even when heavy seas on the quarter tended to slew the hull around.

Sailing dead before the wind, the twin was boomed at twenty-three degrees forward of amidships and in this position was in direct flow, the wind passing from luff to leech.   On this course an increase in the strength of the wind resulted in the sail developing more power, and the tiller would be pulled to weather and held there while the yacht sailed by the lee.   However, before the yacht got far enough around to gybe, the fore-and-aft sails partially would blanket the twin and the yacht would eventually take up a course with the wind at five to ten degrees on the leeward quarter.   An increase in the shockcord tension would quickly bring the yacht back on the set course again.

In light winds it was necessary to secure both the sheet and the shockcord to the inboard end of the tiller—for more sensitivity but, as the wind increased, the sheet was eased aft until, in strong winds,

D'VARA *is a thirty-foot overall main trysail ketch.* She will steer *herself to windward with the tiller free*

it was attached to the middle of the tiller. In the latter position the pull of the sheet on the tiller was halved, and the shockcord tension could be kept within bounds. Although the spinnaker measured only 104 square feet, it developed a pull in heavy going that required the weight of both of us to sheet it in and this gave some indication of the tension that the shockcord was subjected to for days on end.

This system has proved to be entirely reliable and utilizes equipment to be found abroad any cruising yacht. The spinnaker referred to actually looks like a high-clewed jib, the clew being one third of the luff above the tack. The spinnaker pole is socketed to the mast at ten feet above deck, while the tack is shackled to an eyebolt forward and to one side of the mainmast. An additional feature of this sail is its self-stowing qualities ; to strike it in a squall it is only necessary to throw off the halliard and let it run. As the sail comes down, the boom swings the clew forward and inboard and the rest of the sail needs only a gasket to hold it in place.

One advantage of this system over any other is that the steering sail—the weather twin—is contributing to the actual progress of the vessel and there is no elaborate setup of bearings, joints, electrical contacts, etc., which always seem out of place and require special maintenance.

SELF STEERING WITH THE WEATHER TWIN
by Stanley E. Bradfield
(Quotes from letters to Frits Fenger)

Sept. 12th, 1961—*Aden*.

We left Gan on June 3 and expected to find a S.W. Monsoon with a 3 knot easterly set due to the equatorial counter-current setting us well to the east of the Chagos Islands. However, there was no set and the wind was southerly so we fell away on the port tack and left *D'VARA* to find her own way. (That is, close-hauled under working sails). After 5 days of windward work, the breeze went astern, so down the fore and afters and up the twins. However, the wind was only force 3 and we did not make much progress, so I dropped the port twin and hoisted the maintrysail and mizzen. By leading the starboard twin sheet to the tiller and counter-balancing it with shock cord, I got self-steering. After 18 hours, the wind went to S.E. course 180°, so I gybed over and hoisted the port twin and dropped the starboard twin. For the next ten days, *D'VARA* ran off happily before the quartering breeze ; sometimes it even got abeam and worked up to force 5, but a slight adjustment of sheets and shock cord was sufficient to keep her going in the right direction. The wind was actually light most of the way as we were never below 5 south, but then that is better than force 7.

Nov. 1st, 1961—Aden.

We used the weather twin to help steering from the time we left Port Moresby, but it was not until we left the Maldive Islands that I worked out the self-steering properties. Being faced with an 1,100 mile sail across an empty ocean, I had hoped to use the twins, but the wind was on the quarter or even further forward, so that was out. As the twin was up, I shackled a block to the mizzen runner chain plate and led the sheet through this to the tiller. In a force 4 wind, there was considerable pull on the sheet, and this was balanced by rubber cord, the correct tension being found by trial. To my delight, and also my wife's, *D'VARA* maintained a steady course. Later, when the wind went forward, the leech began to shake so I eased the pole forward and the self-steering was maintained.

However, I did find that the tension on the shock cord needed to be varied in different strength winds. In very light winds, it was difficult to get enough weight on the sheet to counteract any pull on the shock cord, but this was finally overcome by using only a very short piece of shock cord, 2 or 3 inches, which, being attached to the end of the tiller, magnified its pull sufficiently to bring the tiller back to a central position but then had no tension left to pull it down to leeward. Perhaps a better designed quarter block would make the difference ?

Even when running dead before the wind, I found that I still had self-steering with this arrangement. In fact, it was possible to lower the main-trysail in heavy winds with no upset to the system. This applied to the wind on the quarter also. When the wind was on the quarter I used the mizzen staysail, but otherwise both staysails were on deck.

Question 1. (At approximately what angles did you sheet your twin). Answer : " When before the wind the twin was sheeted at approximately 23° forward of the beam (it just about touches the lower main shroud in this position). When on the quarter I estimate that the angle was roughly 45°, but this would be varied to keep the leech from shaking, being eased forward if the wind went any further ahead."

Question 2. (How much did the tiller move). Answer: " The tiller tended to move too much so that I limited its movement by using pins in a rail (see sketch). I found that the course could be altered a few degrees by moving one of the pins further in or out, thus limiting the tiller's movement, or increasing it.

Question 3. (How true a course did she sail). Answer : " In steady winds above 5 knots, the course maintained was as good as an average helmsman. In winds above 15 knots I think the course was steadier than a helmsman could manage but this may only apply to my hull." The hull is from the lines of *DREAM OF ARDEN* by Harrison Butler and has an excellent " Metacentric shelf " line— straight for almost its entire length, except for the very ends where it flares slightly.

Question 4. (When sailing with the wind on the quarter, did you use the mizzen-staysail ? And was it stood to weather) : Answer : " Yes to both parts."

In strong winds, the pull on the weather twin sheet was very powerful (augmented by the acute angle when the sail is well forward) and if an adjustment had to be made, I would strain to get it in while Dot would take in the slack on the tiller. Usually, I had the sheet tied to the middle of the tiller and the shock cord to the end. The cord I used was of $\frac{1}{2}$ inch diameter, solid rubber, and is normally used for powering underwater spearguns. In force 3-4 winds I used one piece 9 inches long and had it under tension, and another 6 inches long which only began to stretch when the tiller went to windward or amidships. As the wind increased, I would add another 9 inch length and vary its tension to suit. As the wind fell away, I used only one length and varied this as the breeze got lighter. The sheet was 2 ft. 6 ins. and the shock cord 4 feet from the rudder stock. (Ratio 1 : 1.6).

VANE GEARS

This type of gear is sensitive to changes in wind direction and steers a course relative to the apparent wind as a result. Its method of operation is different from the " sheet to tiller " gears in that it is worked by changes in the wind's direction acting on a vane and not by the variation in force exerted by the wind on the sails. Due to its relatively low power output, however, it will only self steer at its best on a well balanced boat.

Vanes, as wind direction indicators are very old and were doubtless tried by the Dutch to keep their windmills pointing into the wind before the little rotary windmill wheel was invented to keep them steered into position. However, the first reference to a vane gear we have found is in the following letter to *Yachting Monthly* of April, 1919 (page 404).

A Self Steering Device

Dear Sir,—The correspondence in your columns some time ago on the difficulties in the way of making long single-handed passages such as Captain Slocum's has encouraged me to experiment with a self-steering device which I have had in mind for some years. It is diffierent from any used up to the present—as far as I can discover—on either model or full-sized vessels. It is so simple to construct, and has proved so perfect and universal in its action, that I cannot help thinking that a description of it may be of general interest.

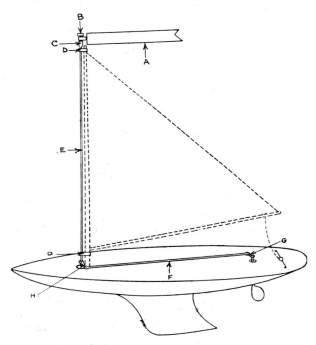

The mechanism is shown in its simple experimental form in the diagram appended. A large vane (A) is mounted on an upright rod or spindle (E), which is parallel to and supported on the mast by two bearers (DD). The vane is so attached to the spindle (E) that it can be moved round and fixed in any required position in a horizontal circle. This is accomplished in my model by threading the top of the spindle, putting on a fixed shoulder (C), and clipping down the ring at the butt end of the vane by a milled tightening nut (B). The lower end of the spindle turns on a metal thrust-plate on the deck.

Close to the deck, there is fixed on the spindle, an arm (H) on the port side, which is connected by a rod (F) with a tiller (G) projecting from the starboard side of the rudder head. (Mast and sail are dotted in.)

The action is as follows :—Clip down the vane in such a position that it will look into the wind's eye when the boat is on the required course with helm steady. Trim sheets and start the boat. It will be found that the wind's action on the vane will give the necessary helm to correct any deviation from the course.

To give the system a stiff test, I constructed a model 36 ins. over all, with a profile roughly like that of Linton Hope's 18 footer in the *Yachting Monthly* of June, 1915. She has a short wooden fin keel, a hanging metal rudder, and is rigged with a single leg-of-mutton sail. She has no steadying after fin like the standard type of short keeled models such as Electra, Prospero etc., which are designed to be steered by the " Braine " system ; but is in all essential respects the same as a full-sized craft below water. The steering vane is of thin wood, about 14 inches by $1\frac{1}{2}$ inches. This is of ample power, and would probably bear cutting down.

I tested this model on the partly excavated Littleton Reservoir, a sheet of water about 400 yards by 150, and the result was surprisingly good, warranting fully the following conclusions :—

1. It corrects deviations on either side of the course on which the boat is laid, and is equally efficient on a pinch to windward and on a dead run to leeward.

2. Though it is possible for the vane to be too small, it cannot be made so powerful as to give over-correction. Therefore it is necessarily more perfectly automatic than any existing system.

3. Being unconnected with the sails, it can be used with any rig, from a dipping lug or other loose-footed sail to a full rigged ship.

4. Being simple, light and taking up little deck space, and its connection, disconnection, and adjustment being done in a moment, it is easily to be adopted for use in a sea-going vessel.

With regard to the last point, it would of course be necessary to arrange the point of control, connection and disconnection within easy reach of the deck. The vane would have to be collapsible, and easily hoisted and lowered. The connection between the spindle and the tiller would be by wire lines leading along the sides of the deck through suitable blocks. I am confident that neither of these variations presents any really serious difficulty.

H. Hambley Tregoning.

Thames United Sailing Club.

(We have an idea that the ingenious device described above has already been tried in model sailing.—Ed. Yachting Monthly 1919).

Since this letter was written in 1919, model yachtsmen have accumulated a lot of data about vane gears which is of value to the sailor and, before considering the design of vane gears for full sized yachts, a description of the model vane gears and the main principles of design is necessary. Mr. A. Wilcock, who is a keen model yachtsman and a successful designer of vane gears, has given us valuable assistance by placing his material and his experience at our disposal.

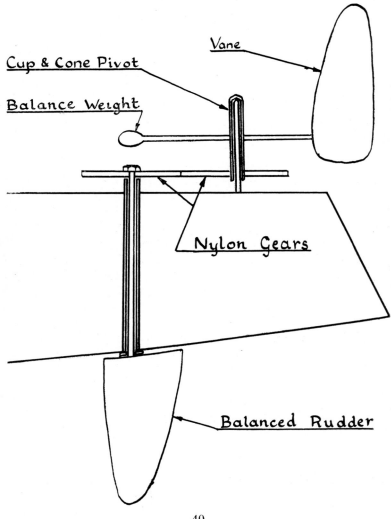

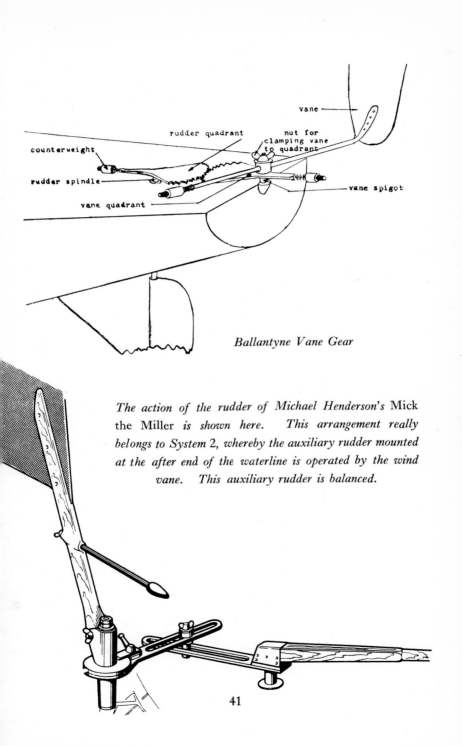

vane

rudder quadrant

nut for
clamping vane
to quadrant

counterweight

rudder spindle

vane spigot

vane quadrant

Ballantyne Vane Gear

The action of the rudder of Michael Henderson's Mick
the Miller *is shown here. This arrangement really
belongs to System 2, whereby the auxiliary rudder mounted
at the after end of the waterline is operated by the wind
vane. This auxiliary rudder is balanced.*

The model vane gear falls into two main categories, the difference between them being in the design of the linkage connecting the vane and the rudder. The first of these is two meshing cog wheels as in the drawing by G. F. H. Singleton and its handier version " The moving carriage gear ". A lighter version is the Ballantyne gear which uses the same system of interlocking cog wheels but cuts some of them away. The second system is the Fisher gear which uses slotted bars interlocking through a pivot.

THE " MOVING CARRIAGE GEAR "

This system has been developed by Mr. Wilcock from the idea first produced by Marin Marie as an effective and useful model gear. In its simplest form, it consists of a gear wheel mounted on top of the rudder spindle meshing with a gear wheel carrying the vane. Both gears are of the same size. The vane and its gear wheel are mounted

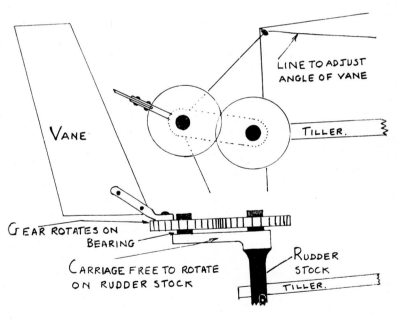

on a carriage which is free to rotate on the rudder spindle, the two gears thereby staying in mesh when the carriage rotates. The vane angle relative to the rudder (and thus the course of the boat to the apparent wind) is set by rotating the carriage at half the angle at which vane rotation is desired, for instance, if the carriage is rotated through 45°, the vane will rotate through 90°. Movement of the carriage permits precise, rapid and accurate adjustment of the angle.

On the fully engineered model vane, the carriage forms part of the vane assembly so that the vane can be positioned well clear of the sails. Connection from the carriage spindle to the rudder is by yokes and links. The carriage swings between adjustable stops to permit automatic tacking, and sheets can be led to the carriage to trigger off manoeuvres such as gybing.

A moving carriage gear would increase the handiness of nearly all the full sized vane gears at present used to allow for continuous and fine course setting with the full sized yacht under way. The " Herbert " and " Morwood " gears, described later, are gears of the " moving carriage " type which use vanes mounted on horizontal axles.

The model yacht's vane is pivoted on needle point bearings and is linked to the tiller so that a clockwise rotation of the vane causes an anti-clockwise rotation of the rudder. If, for example, the apparent wind direction changes and blows more from the beam, the vane will swing more outboard, causing the rudder to turn the boat into the wind until it is back on course. If the apparent wind draws ahead, the vane swings inboard and the rudder turns the boat off the wind. The angle of the vane relative to the fore and aft line of the boat can be adjusted for the course to be sailed.

The vane gear used on models is extremely sensitive, the vane responding to the slightest puff of wind. Each component is carefully counterbalanced to ensure that the helm is not affected by gravitational effects when the boat is heeled. The rudder and vane pivots are made as friction-free as possible because the variations in power which the vane is capable of passing on to the rudder are extremely small compared to the power available from the sheet to tiller gears. Indeed, much of the development work on these gears has centered around the problem of getting the most use of the limited power available.

The basic design features are given below. They are the result of the experiments of the model yachting fraternity on both sides of the Atlantic. They relate in general to models with the " canoe body " type of hull with " fin and bulb " keel with separate rudder. However, the vane gear has also been successfully used on " full keel " models.

THE VANE DESIGN

Area :   4 to 6 times the rudder area.
Cross section : Symmetrical aerofoil whose maximum thickness is one third of the chord from the leading edge.

Shape :   Rectangular with roundings. Span to chord between
                     4 : 1 and 6 : 1.
Weight :   As light as possible, generally balsa wood.

The vane is mounted almost vertically, generally with its leading
edge parallel with the mast. It should be positioned as far away from
the backwinding effects of the sails as possible. The vane seems always
to be mounted so as to rotate around a vertical axis, though more
power could be derived from a near-horizontal axis as with *PEN
DUICK'S* gear, described later.

The distance from the centre of the vane area to the vane pivot
is twice as long as the forward pointing vane arm, thus giving a
mechanical advantage of 2 : 1. The rudder arm (or aft-pointing tiller)
is also twice the length of the vane arm with which it engages. The
vane force is therefore multiplied by four as a turning force on the
rudder. In the Fisher gear, this mechanical advantage is adjustable to
cope with the differences in the apparent wind speeds between the
close hauled and running courses. The vane is counterbalanced by a
weight to avoid rotation on heeling.

THE RUDDER DESIGN

Area :   4 to 4½% of the total lateral area.
Shape :   At least twice as deep as it is wide. The rudder
                     skeg should be deep and narrow also.

The rudder should be placed well aft so that it has the maximum
effect and must be counterbalanced to avoid the effects of gravity and
buoyancy. The rudder pivots must be as friction-free as possible and
there must be adequate clearance in the rudder trunk to avoid binding.
Model yacht rudders are seldom " balanced ".

THE MODEL SAILING TECHNIQUE

The vane gear is balanced up by adjusting the counterweights with
the boat in the water at various angles of heel. The gear is then made
inoperative while the sailing balance of the boat is checked. The sail
plan is adjusted so that, in a light breeze, the boat will sail to windward
with the helm free. Having achieved this, the mast is moved slightly
aft so that the boat carries slight weather helm. By doing this, the
vane is given a slight " angle of attack " to the wind when the boat is
on course, which ensures that the power variations of the vane with
changes in the wind direction are strongest.

To explain this point, let us assume that the boat is tuned so
that no helm is needed to keep it on a close-hauled course. The vane,

being unloaded, will then fly freely in line with the apparent wind. Now, the vane has to be a symmetrical aerofoil so that it can work equally well on both tacks and a symmetrical aerofoil does not generate any appreciable force until its angle of attack becomes about 5° from the direction of the airflow. Thus, the wind direction can vary 5° either way before the vane starts applying correcting helm. This blind spot reduces the sensitivity of the gear and the performance of the boat noticeably and weather helm is deliberately introduced to load the vane and prevent this. The graph illustrates the sort of power variations which can be expected from a vane having a symmetrical aerofoil section.

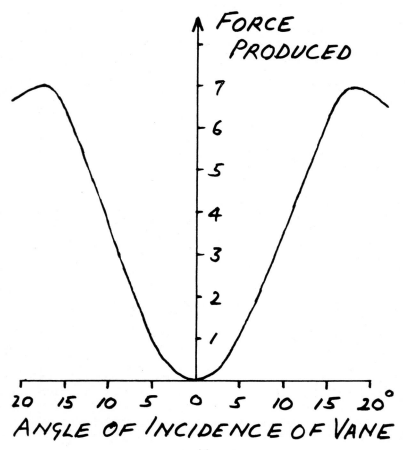

To sail a course, the boat is pointed on the course to be sailed and the sails are trimmed. The vane is unclamped and allowed to swing freely when it will point into the *True* wind. It is then swung inboard a few degrees to allow for the apparent wind angle being less than the true wind angle and it is clamped. The boat is then released and, as it sails off, the vane swings inboard due to the wind flow past it and applies weather helm to keep the boat on course.

Like all aerofoils, the lift obtained from the vane will increase as its angle of attack increases until the " stalling point " is reached. In the case of this type of vane, that angle will be about 18°. The angle of attack which the vane adopts, with the boat on course, will depend on the load imposed by the rudder. The greater the load, the nearer will the vane be to stalling. Now, if the vane is working near the stalling angle, its control over the boat is limited because an increase in the angle of attack, due to a change in wind direction, will stall the vane which cannot then produce the extra power needed to correct the boat's heading. For this reason, the power needed to correct the boat's course must be kept small and well within the capability of the vane. Hence the need for the boat to be well balanced and the rudder to be designed to suit the vane (by balancing it, for example).

When a vane stalls it usually flutters due to the breakaway of the airflow on the lee side and its power output falls. The power output can, however, be improved by making the vane rotate around an axis sloped up at about 10° from the horizontal. When this is done, a windshift in direction will cause far more vane movement about a longer lever arm and thus be capable of producing far more power and work. It begins to resemble the " windmill " gear, described later. Even if such a vane is driven to its utmost extent when it will be roughly horizontal, its angle of incidence will not be more than the 10° of its axle.

VANE STEERING FOR FULL SIZED YACHTS

History. The first use of vane steering aboard a full sized yacht to our knowledge was in 1936 by the celebrated French yachtsman and artist, Marin Marie for his motor yacht *ARIELLE*. His invention of twin foresails for Trade Wind sailing has already been mentioned but for a single-handed crossing of the Atlantic under power, he had to devise some method for steering while he slept. The photograph of *ARIELLE* and his sketches of his gears show his thoughts on the subject. The sketch on the extreme right, subsequently labelled " The Moving Carriage Gear " by Wilcock, seems to be the one

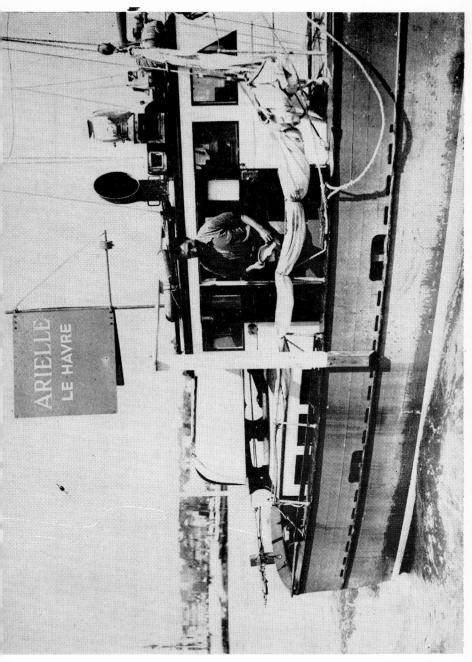

..in Marie on his arrival at Le Havre after a transtalantic passage in Arielle. _From_
..d vanes and gear that gave some trouble, he eventually evolved a compact gear acting
direct on the rudder that proved suitable for power boats or sailing boats

preferred by Marin Marie and this is not surprising because the course can be set while the vane is actually steering the boat by rotating the top bearings and, if a grooved wheel were to be mounted around them, a line around it with both ends being taken to the cockpit would

Here are *Arielle's* Remote Control Arrangements

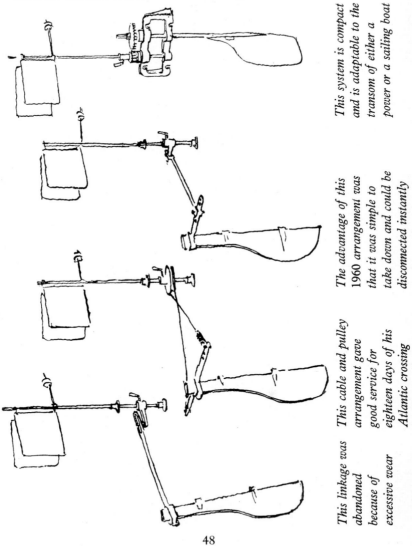

This system is compact and is adaptable to the transom of either a power or a sailing boat

The advantage of this 1960 arrangement was that it was simple to take down and could be disconnected instantly

This cable and pulley arrangement gave good service for eighteen days of his Atlantic crossing

This linkage was abandoned because of excessive wear

allow full control of the yacht at all times when sailing without touching (or perhaps even *Needing*) the tiller.

ARIELLE'S Atlantic crossing was successful and it proved that vane self steering could work. Marin Marie's book *Wind Aloft, Wind Alow*, describing his solo Atlantic crossings with both the twins and the vane is one of the yachting classics. But such is the conservative nature of yachtsmen that it was not until the mid 1950's that self steering gears, using vanes, were again used.

The next application we know of was by Ian Major who, in 1955, fitted his twin-keeled yacht *BUTTERCUP* with the gear shown, and made a successful crossing to the West Indies. This gear is believed to have been the first " trim-tab " gear ever fitted to a full sized boat, and the first to incorporate a " Differential Linkage " (see below).

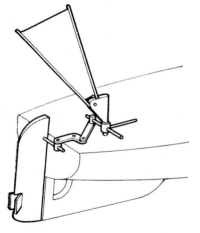

Buttercup's *rudder. The wind vane operates trim tabs on the main rudder*

He based his design on the results of his own model trials in previous years. Here, the vane consisted of two rods with canvas between them. Its area could therefore be easily varied and quickly stowed. This vane acts on the end of a lever (with several bearings in it to allow for course setting) which turns about a single bearing in the deck. The after end works a push-pull rod in the fore part of the rudder stock. The mechanism is not perfectly clear, but we think that the trim tab on the rudder has a small tiller of its own at the top of the rudder and the push-pull rod works this. The use of a small tiller on the trim tab provides the " Differential Linkage " which will be described more fully later. If the boat is going close-hauled and the wind comes more abeam, the vane is pressed to leeward. This pulls the push-pull rod to windward which sets the trim-tab to lee and the

Mick the Miller *with her self steering gear in use.* (*Photo: Beken, Cowes*)

water flow pushes the rudder up to windward, luffing the yacht.   Col.
Hasler has written to us stating that he did not have any part in designing *BUTTERCUP'S* gear, as stated in one of the articles cn the
subject.

Marin Marie's *ARIELLE* self steering gear was well known.
The *BUTTERCUP* gear was seen but the method of operation was
shrouded in some sort of a mystery—perhaps because the concepts
were too new for us to understand them.   It was therefore fortunate
that in 1955, Michael Henderson fitted a full sized Fisher gear to
MICK THE MILLER, his J.O.G. yacht and sailed her throughout
the 1955 sailing season with such success that we knew that self steering
for full sized yachts had " arrived ".

" HARRIET," THE THIRD HAND ON *MICK THE MILLER*

MICK THE MILLER is a 17 foot waterline Junior Offshore
Group racing boat, cutter rigged.   As shown in Fig. 1, she is fitted
with two rudders.   The main rudder is hung on the trailing edge of the
fin keel and a small balanced rudder of 1.4 square feet is hung on a
skeg at the aft end of the waterline.   The balancing area of the rudder
is 17%.   " Harriet " a Fisher type vane gear is coupled to the small
balanced rudder when self steering is required.

The vane is a piece of 1/8th inch plywood 2.43 square feet in
area and is counterbalanced against the effects of gravity when heeled.
It swings on a spigot on the transom and can be taken off and kept
below when on moorings.   As shown in Fig. 1, the vane can be
clamped to the vane arm at any desired angle and movements of the
vane are transmitted to the rudder via the adjustable pin on the vane
arm.   This allows the pin position to be adjusted to alter the mechanical advantage of the vane over the rudder.

The action of the gear is similar to the model vane gear, described
earlier.   A full description of " Harriet " appeared in a very interesting article in the April 1957 *Yachting World* to whose Editor we
are indebted for the loan of the blocks for the drawings of *Mick's*
gear and for Michael Henderson's drawings of alternative methods
of self steering (Fig. 2).

Michael Henderson, " Harriet's " designer, writes of her : " I
don't think there is anything magic about the proportions of the rig.
Mick's balanced rudder was exactly balanced in practice but I fancy
that a trifle of unbalance would be better, just enough to centralise
the helm.   The vane area was just drawn until it looked right and I
took two slices off after it was fitted until it looked neat but still worked.

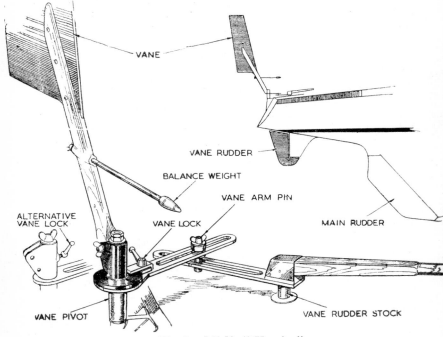

VANE

VANE RUDDER

BALANCE WEIGHT

VANE ARM PIN

ALTERNATIVE
VANE LOCK

VANE LOCK

MAIN RUDDER

VANE PIVOT

VANE RUDDER STOCK

Fig. 1   *Mick's " Harriet "*

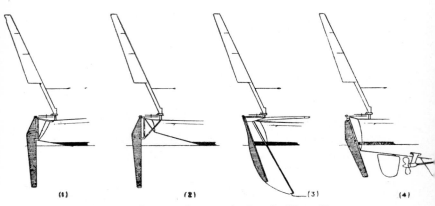

(1)   (2)   (3)   (4)

Fig. 2   *Suggested ways of using the Vane Gear*

" The great need is absolute freedom of movement. Not only must friction be eliminated but so must any tendency to stick. These requirements can be met by using nicely polished *Tufnol* bearings with lots and lots of slop. *Mick* has ¾ inch bore bearings running on 5/8th inch spindles, for both rudder and vane. In a sea way, the whole assembly can rattle gently on its mountings and has no tendency to stick.

" The vane gear was finished and fitted in 1955 and, with its assistance, we were able to win the J.O.G. championship that year. There is no possible doubt that ' Harriet ' has had a very great effect on *Mick's* success. In all offshore racing and particularly the J.O.G., crew comfort and lack of fatigue is at least 50% of the total ' raceability.' In J.O.G., one can almost reverse the old saw and say that the best cruiser is the best racer and the vane does indeed reduce the burden of watchkeeping on one hand and, what is more, is able to steer a far better course than most humans especially to windward and at night. A spell of 20 hours at the helm has no effect on that accuracy. In bad weather, it is equally a help.

" Two instances will show the value of Harriet :

" (1) John Hetherington brought the boat back from Cherbourg just after Whitsun last year (1956) and averaged 4¾ knots to windward across the channel in winds which were reported to be between force 6 and 7. He set ' Harriet ' off Barfleur and retired below in the dry while *Mick* gave her celebrated impression of a submarine. Apart from periodic visits on deck to see that no steamers were getting too intimate, he remained below until having to tack off St. Catherines.

" (2) In 1955, I brought *Mick* back from Falmouth to Portsmouth at the end of our holiday, close-hauled all the way in force 4 most of the time, 60 hours from port to port, and we literally steered out of Falmouth and into Portsmouth. Apart from tacking times, ' Harriet ' had her ! "

John Hetherington, who owned *MICK THE MILLER* during the 1956 season writes : " The vane gear is worth an extra hand at all times. On long passages, it considerably reduced the effort required as the steering could be left to the vane and the crew were able to carry out their other tasks and obtain a sufficient amount of sleep. The vane gear was used by myself during the 1956 season when the winds came quite strong on occasions. There was no failure of the gear whatsoever, either mechanically or in its operation."

Bernard Moitessier. This ocean cruising Frenchman became interested in self steering gears in 1957 and fitted his *MARIE-THERESE* and Henri Wakelam's *WANDA* with self steering vane

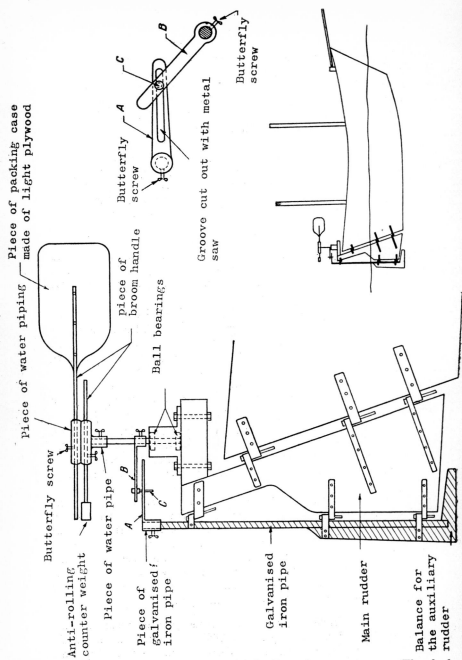

Piece of packing case
made of light plywood

Butterfly
screw

Groove cut out with metal
saw

Butterfly
screw

Piece of water piping

piece of
broom handle

Ball bearings

Butterfly screw

Anti-rolling
counter weight

Piece of water pipe

Piece of
galvanised
iron pipe

Galvanised
iron pipe

Main rudder

Balance for
the auxiliary
rudder

As long ago as 1957 two deep sea cruisers fitted self steering arrangements. They had re
about them and they devised them from what materials they could lay their hands
easily.   Note that the sketch is obviously wrong in the angle of the pintle on the rude
head

gears acting through Fisher gears on what look like trim tabs but are, in fact, small rudders. We are publishing the diagram we have of the system. In this case, the rudder is fixed which puts excessive strains on it, as mentioned by Peter Tangvald in our publication *Solo Cruising*, whereas a free-swinging rudder controlled by a trim-tab is much less likely to be overstrained.

Jean Lacombe. On *GOLIF* in the 1964 Solo Trans-Atlantic race, Jean Lacombe had a curious gear with two alternative linkages. Either the vane could be linked to the trim-tab through a Fisher linkage

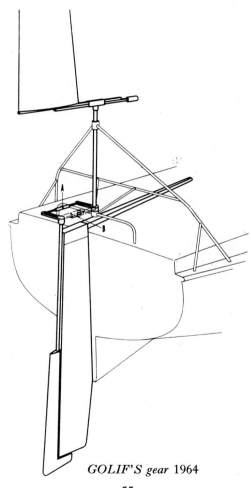

GOLIF'S gear 1964

with the rudder fixed, thus giving a Moitessier system.   Or, the rudder could be allowed to swing freely and the vane could work the trim-tab directly, thus giving the ordinary servo trim-tab mechanism.

THE DESIGN PRINCIPLES OF FULL SIZED VANE GEARS

As compared with model yachts, it is not really possible to set a large enough vane to work a normal rudder, except possibly on multi-hulls.   Francis Chichester used what was virtually a large mizzen to

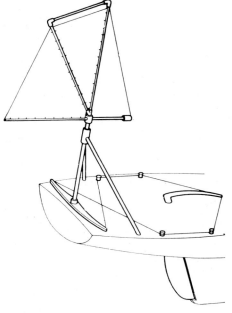

Here's how Francis Chichester's wind vane was linked to and operated the main rudder's tiller

work his rudder in two of his Atlantic crossings in 1960 and 1962 which he called " Miranda " and practically worshipped but one thinks it must have been a bit of a beast at times.   In order to reduce the size of the vane, the following methods have been used :—
1.   The rudder can be balanced.
2.   A separate small rudder can be mounted aft of the main rudder and fitted with a self steering gear.   See : *MICK THE MILLER.*
3.   The rudder can be fixed and the vane made to work a trim-tab which actually steers the boat as in the Moitessier gear.
4.   The main rudder can be fitted with a " servo " trim-tab, controlled by the vane.   This servo then steers the main rudder which, in turn, steers the boat.

56

5. The main rudder can be controlled by an athwartships swinging "Pendulum" through running lines. The angle of incidence of the "Pendulum" is set by the vane. See : Hasler gears.

6. The vane can revolve around an axis sloped at about 10° from the horizontal as in *PEN DUICK'S* gear.

7. A windmill gear can be used converting energy from the wind flow to steering.

The working of all these gears is more or less self explanatory, once one has appreciated the basic principles of self steering and seen the drawings. Some, such as the windmill gear have never had a good try out on a boat while others, such as the *PEN DUICK* gear have not been tried enough. One feature, which should be included in

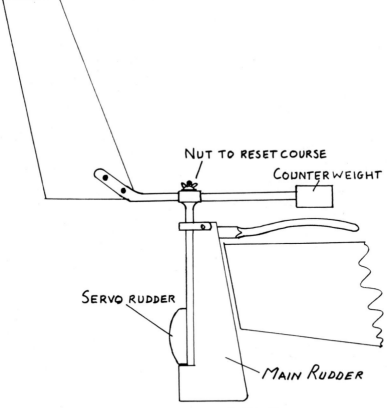

Fig. 1 *A Servo Controlled Rudder*

57

many of the gears needs comment. This is called " The Differential Linkage ".

The Differential Linkage. Fig. 1 shows the simplest form of vane-servo-tab which will give self steering and it has not got a

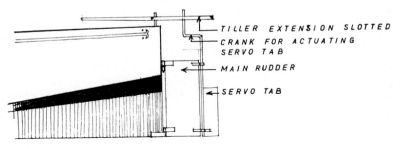

TILLER EXTENSION SLOTTED

CRANK FOR ACTUATING
SERVO TAB

MAIN RUDDER

SERVO TAB

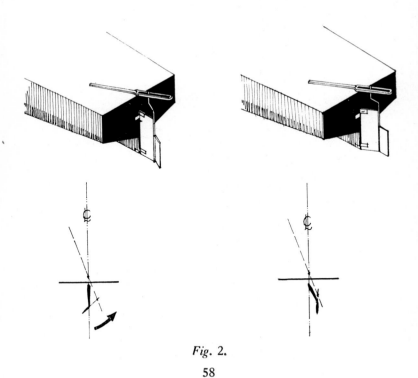

Fig. 2.

" differential linkage." It has the disadvantage, however, that, as the main rudder swings over in response to the servo-tab movement, the angle between the servo-tab and the main rudder will increase, resulting in violent and unstable steering. Therefore, most servo actuated vane gears put this differential linkage between the vane and the servo to ensure that the response to servo-tab movement is steady and stable.

The basic principle of the differential linkage is shown in a very simple form in Fig. 2. The servo-tab has a forward facing tiller with a crank in it which is here actuated by a slotted extension. As the tiller is moved, the servo-tab is turned by the crank and servo-tiller. The waterflow then makes the rudder follow the tiller. As the rudder angle gets near that of the tiller extension, the servo-tab angle is reduced by the crank and servo-tiller. Eventually, the servo-tab will settle down almost in line with the rudder though, of course, a slight angle is needed to hold the rudder at an angle. A further explanation of the differential linkage is given by Marcel Gianoli in the article which follows which concerns the design of Jean Lacombe's gear for the 1960 Solo Trans-Atlantic Race.

AUTOMATIC COURSE STABILISER
BY MARCEL GIANOLI

Principles

" Without undue risk, we wish to allow the helmsman to leave the tiller, while the boat maintains a given heading in relation to the wind.

" The wind-vane, usually thought of merely as an indicator, is here the simplest of heading pointers. If it is of appreciable size it can produce, according to the boat's heading and the direction of the wind, sufficient power to operate a simple Servo-mechanism, which, when linked with the rudder in such a way as to counteract deviation, can become a course stabiliser.

" This Servo-mechanism, though simple, is capable of transforming the slight governing movements of the vane and consists of an articulated tab on the trailing edge of the rudder blade. The tab obtains its energy from its passage through the water, and, when hydrodynamically balanced, is easily controlled by the vane.

" We can see on the diagram that if the angle of a relative wind V turns through angle A, the vane will pivot through an angle B (slightly the lesser because of resistance). The tab will turn in the same direction through an angle C which is defined by the product ($D \times C = D \times B$). The tab is thus subjected to hydrodynamic reaction F which drags the rudder through an angle E. Equilibrium is reached when the equal and opposite force G on the rudder balance that of the tab, or : F x a = G x b.

"The tab lever, a, being greater than the rudder lever b, G is greater than F and the difference, G—F, makes the boat turn to H and so reduces the initial deviation A. This correction will cease when turning the boat to H has compensated the wind deviation A and the course will then be regained relative to the wind.

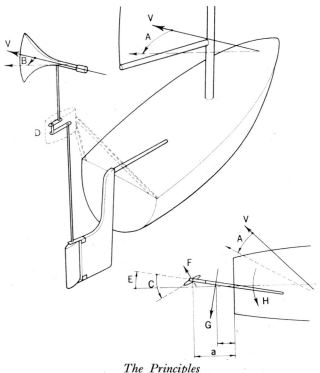

The Principles
Above : Diagrammatic explanation of the principles of a wind vane operated trim tab. (See text for explanation.)

"However, in this process of automatic steering, the turning inertia of the vessel intervenes—an upsetting factor. Even when the rudder comes fore and aft at the same time as the deviation A is cancelled, the boat swings past the point of balance and oscillations are set up. Meanwhile the hull is subjected to the damping factor of water resistance, and as the inertias are tied to the square of the turning speed, and the damping elements only to the speed itself, the oscillations will be weakened if their values are small and increase if they are large.

"Thus a small amount of helm will bring a boat slowly on to her proper heading where she will steady, while if a lot of helm is applied at the beginning of the manoeuvre, she will swing past her correct heading.

"It is to remedy this characteristic that the adjustable reduction mechanism shown in the diagram has been devised. A small value D, which only turns the tab a fraction of the deviation of the wind, will give the best linkage between the vane and the tab—it will correct quickly enough without setting up unwanted oscillations. This adjustment is made when the stabiliser is fitted to a given boat, and it should be simple to change it to suit varying wind strengths, because this influences the speed of the boat, and therefore the efficiency of the rudder."

Equipment made for Jean Lacombe

"Robert Boname, having entrusted Jean Lacombe with one of the *CAP HORNS* that the imports into the United States set us the problem well before the start of the Singlehanded Transatlantic Race but the final design was ready a mere six weeks before the start.

"Fortunately we had, by then, already taken the first steps in the automatic steering of aircraft by means of vanes, so it was possible, fairly quickly, to suggest an adaptation for a sailing vessel. M.N.O.P. managed to make drawings of this suggestion, and to manufacture and install the gear in record time.

"It seemed that some experiment was going to be required with the possible vane areas (5, 10 and 15 sq. ft.), and with the reduction from vane to tab angle (D = 0.33, 0.5 and 1.0). As it happened there was not even time to give the gear a preliminary trial on the Seine, so to be on the safe side, the powerful vane of 15 sq. ft. area was used and coupled with the big reduction of 0.33.

"On the first third of the crossing to America with fairly steady winds, the steering gear proved most efficient, and on several occasions it was possible to leave the helm for periods of up to 24 hours. Later, however, some irregularities appeared, the adjustment changing for no apparent reason.

"Finally, about two-thirds of the way across the gear seized and this was because in the rush to get ready, the anti-fouling of rudder and tab had been overlooked and subsequent weed growth had jammed the system. When the gear was examined after the trip, it was found

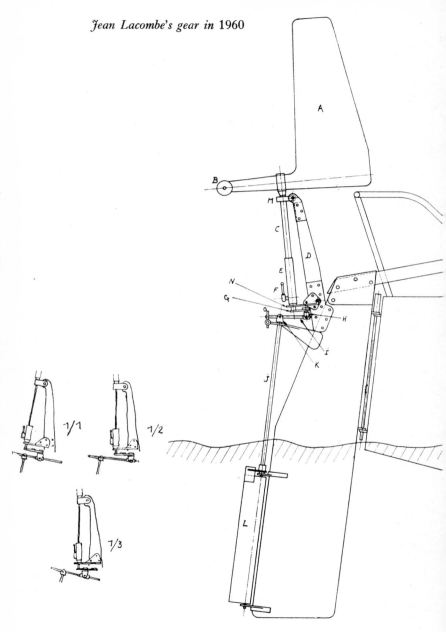

Jean Lacombe's gear in 1960

The Arrangement

A general arrangement drawing of the fittings necessary to operate a trim tab, which in turn operates the main rudder.

The wind vane A, balanced by a counterweight B, is fitted on a primary axle C, turning within the mounting D, which is fitted to the rudder. This axle engages in the sleeve E and can be made one with it by tightening the clamp F. This sleeve is provided with an arm G at the end of which is a fork which slides on the tubular arm I, which is operated by axle C.

The arm I is mounted at the end of a second axle J, harnessed in K to the tab L. The two bearings of the axle C : the upper one M and the lower N, allow the axle to take up two different positions about the mounting of M, depending on which holes are being used in N's mounting. This choice determines on I the position of the point of pressure on H— that is to say the reduction of the transmission of movement of the vane to the tab.

A tumbling clear O permits the locking of the tab L at amidships: we can also declutch the vane and resume manual steering.

---

that the stud joining the stem of the tab to the shaft of the vane had scored badly. The friction between these parts accounted for the irregularities half-way across."

Standard Equipment

The course stabiliser meant for the singlehanded sailor will also be of interest to the cruising man, but it is essential that he be offered gear which is efficient, not too bulky, and also reasonably priced and simple to install and maintain. The primary reason against producing a standard self steering gear as a commercial proposition, is that there exists such a tremendous amount of variation in the types of hull to which the gear might be fitted. This problem must be overcome before equipment can be manufactured which is within the scope of the average cruising man.

A second major obstacle which has yet to be satisfactorily overcome is that of being able to vary the area of the vane, for a vane of an area designed for moderate winds will oversteer the boat in stronger winds, and vice versa. It is possible to ease the situation by adjusting the reduction between vane and tab, but in light winds, when it is necessary to use a lot of helm, decreasing the reduction is outside the scope of a moderate sized vane.

To sum up, here are four basic requirements which, through experience, it has been found necessary to satisfy before a self-steering gear can become a generally acceptable commercial proposition for sale as a standard " off-the-peg " piece of equipment :—

1. Vane to be of adjustable area.
2. A transmission unit from the vane with adjustable reduction, a clutch for the vane and a tab locking device.
3. A receiving unit at the tab mounted on the rudder.
4. Flexible transmission.

A SIMPLIFIELD " MILL " GEAR
BY JOHN MORWOOD

For our very first publication on self steering, I made the suggestion that the gear used to steer windmills be used on a boat. This has been criticised as being liable to oversteer and slow to respond. Now that the vane pivoted on a *Horizontal* axis, as described later in this publication is coming to the fore, which, after all is merely the same idea but in a small part, I think we should take another look at the mill gear.

The drawing shows my present ideas on the mill gear. It can be mounted anywhere, of course, where the wind is relatively undisturbed

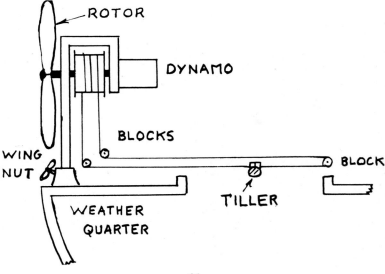

but the weather quarter seems to be best. The drawing is self explanatory and by varying the size of the drum, the gear must work as well as any other. If the drum is too small, the power is very great but oversteer could occur. If too large, the gear will be weak. However, as opposed to all other vanes in this book, the work available is infinite.

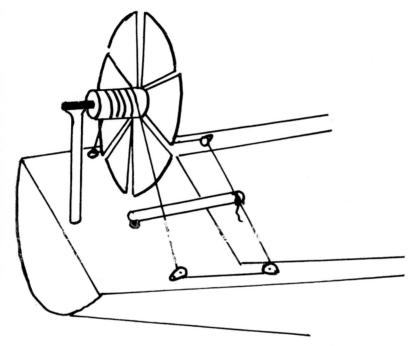

The value of this gear is that " fine " course adjustment is easily possible, and indeed one could actually *Steer* by fixing a tiller to the upright on the windmill. The gear could be instantaneously disengaged by using jamb cleats on the tiller, and slipping out the line.

On a long voyage, two rotors could be carried and the one which is not steering the boat could be used to produce electricity. In harbour, both could be employed thus.

SELF STEERING GEARS IN OCEAN RACING

The 1960 *Solo Trans-Atlantic Race.* This race is properly described as " The Single-handed Transatlantic Race for the Observer

Trophy ". It marks the beginning of an epoch of long distance short handed yacht racing—a type not previously known.   To us, it finally set the seal on the usefulness and even the respectability of self steering.   Francis Chichester's and Jean Lacombe's gears have already been described.   David Lewis and Valentine Howells both used a directly coupled vane-to-trim-tab while Blondie Hasler used a gear with a differential linkage.

The 1964 Solo Trans-Atlantic Race.   This race produced Blondie Hasler's " Swinging pendulum " gear, vane to servo gears with differential linkage and direct vane to servo in all of the 15 yachts

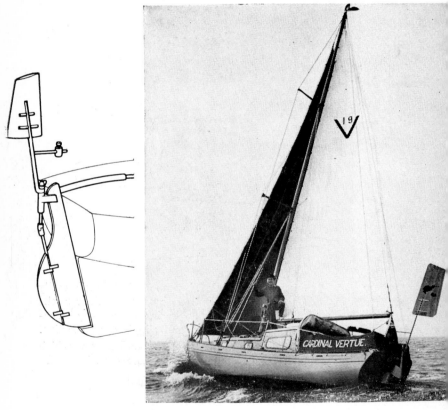

Dr. Lewis's single handled Transatlantic entry Cardinal Vertue *had a vane operated trim tab that was really a part of the main rudder.* 1960.
(*Photo: Eileen Ramsay*)

which sailed. Many of them broke or ceased to function as could be expected with such a new idea. By this time, the Hasler gears had been made commercially and of the 15 starters, 6 boats (*AKKA, LIVELY LADY, JESTER, ILALA, ERICHT, TAMMY NORIE*)

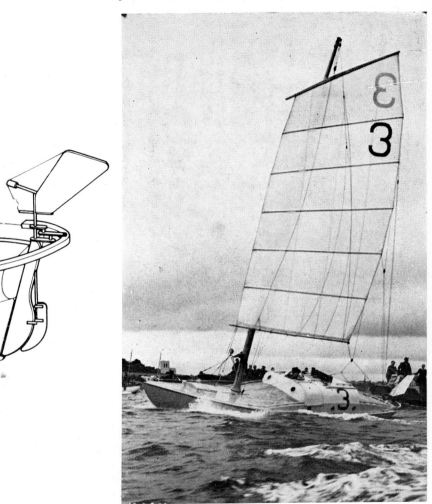

Jester, *"Blondie" Hasler's entry with its adaptation of the Chinese lug-sail, had a wind vane that operated a large trim tab on the after edge of the main rudder. 1960.*   (*Photo: Eileen Ramsay*)

had Hasler " Pendulum servo gears " and one boat (*STARDRIFT*) had an early trim-tab designed by Hasler.

The 1966 *Round Britain Race.* This was a race for a two man crew but self steering again was very desirable and allowed by the rules so a variety of gears appeared on most of the yachts. The Henderson " Running line gear " made its appearance with a variety of other gears of types already described.

Howell's transatlantic entry also had a wind vane operating an auxiliary rudder in 1960.   (*Photo : Eileen Ramsay*)

SELF STEERING GEARS IN 1966

In 1966, sheet to tiller gears seem to have quite gone out of fashion and vanes hold the field for the moment. But the hard school of passage making and ocean crossings will soon cause the unseaworthy gears to vanish, leaving the field to those methods or gears which are simple and reliable and which can steer a steady and good course.

The A.Y.R.S. we think is fully qualified to describe things and even conjecture the most wild and impractical ideas. Our ingenious members seem to be able to make these ideas practical and even seaworthy, like the catamaran, the trimaran and the hydrofoil for stabilising boats or even lifting them off the water. But we would think ourselves foolhardy if we were to guess which of the many systems we describe in this booklet will eventually conquer the field of self steering.

A variety of the most recent self steering vane gears will now be described, all of which use the principles we have shown to exist in the previous pages. Most of them are commercially available or can be custom built for any yacht.

THE HENDERSON GEARS

Mike Henderson's self steering gears are always simple, and effective as well as the smallest possible. This is not surprising as his experience goes back to a full racing season in 1955—the year the A.Y.R.S. started. He has sent us the design drawings of four of them which are as follows :

1. Running line gear to the tillers via quarter blocks as fitted in the Prout *RANGER* and *SEA RANGER* catamarans.

2. Running line gear to tiller via quarter blocks as fitted to *HORIZON*.

3. A vane to trim-tab as fitted to *TWISTER*.

4. A Fisher gear on a partially balanced auxiliary rudder.

The RANGER Gear. This design is of great technical interest because it shows that a small vane of 6-8 square feet can supply enough power to operate two rudders whose combined area exceeds that of the vane. This is possible because a well designed and properly tuned catamaran is light on the helm and docile under all reasonable weather conditions.

We doubt if the vane area used here would be effective on a conventional yacht without either a balanced rudder or servo assistance because of the greater helm corrections needed to overcome the effects of heeling.

Roland Prout writes :

Dear Tom,

This particular design of self steering gear was drawn for a Mr. J. Andrews of Belfast by Mike Henderson for his 27 foot *RANGER* catamaran which he ordered and had delivered last Spring. The steering gear was first used during the delivery sail of this catamaran *TWIN TAIL* from Canvey Island to Belfast, in Northern Ireland.

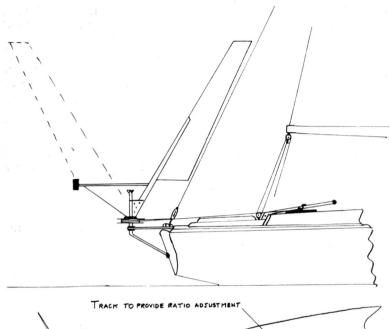

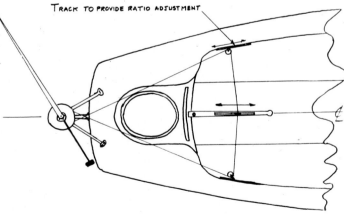

TRACK TO PROVIDE RATIO ADJUSTMENT

Henderson running line gear, yacht HORIZON

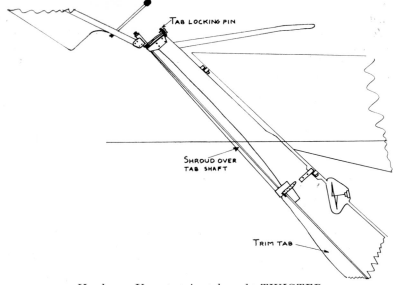

Henderson Vane to trim-tab yacht TWISTER

I sailed with Mr. Andrews from Canvey Island in Essex to Dartmouth in Devon and we used the self steering vane all the time.

The principle of this gear is a plywood vane fitted to a channelled drum approximately 1 foot in diameter, working on a vertical brass spindle. It is balanced by lead weights on a rod extending forward. A continuous terylene (dacron) cord is wound about five times around the drum, and passes via four pulley blocks along the tiller " truss " bar. On the centre of the truss bar are two jamb cleats opposite each other so that the cord can be locked to the bar in any position.

In operation, all that is necessary is for the helmsman to steer the craft on course, allowing the vane to rotate freely into the wind and, when on course, push the cord into the jamb cleats. The vane and tillers are now locked together and the boat is steered relative to the direction of the wind.

The absence of heel and fine balance of helm possible with a well designed catamaran helps to make this vane successful, and only slight adjustments in the position of the cord on the cross bar are necessary to take up the " push " of slight weather helm.

On the cruise I had from Canvey Island to Dartmouth, we allowed the steering vane to take the boat on almost the whole trip, and although fairly frequent attention to slight adjustment of the vane is necessary to steer a true compass course, this is no hardship and we all agreed that the vane was better than another very conscientious crew man. We could not fault the arrangement, and perhaps the only improvement I shall make on my own steering gear is to make some kind of screw adjustment movement on the jamb blocks for fine adjustment after the vane has been " locked-in " to the tillers.

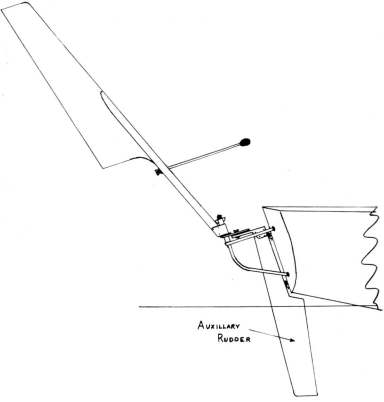

Henderson-Fisher gear

The vane would take over in quite light winds, but very positive steering was possible in all winds from about 7 m.p.h. upwards. Running down a steep sea is a slight problem when the surfing speed of the cat may sometimes take all wind from the vane and in some conditions it will be found necessary to resort to hand steering.

If, as we often are placed, one can only spare one person at a time on watch, the self steering is invaluable. It enables the man on watch to move freely about the craft, make tea, look at the chart, play with the R.T. etc., and his watch period goes much faster.

The self steering vane can be adjusted to keep the boat in a " hove-to " position, or " sailing easily " position in very strong weather or when sails have to be reefed or changed. It can also be made to tack the boat by swinging the vane around through 90° and re-jamming the terylene line on the cleats, thus allowing this manoeuvre to be done by one person who is then free to change sheets and re-adjust the sails without the need to touch the helm.

ROLAND PROUT.

1, The Point, Canvey Island, Essex.

HASLER WIND VANES
BY M. S. GIBB LTD.,
Warsash, Hampshire, England

How They Started

(1) Wind-Vane Steering Gear for sailing yachts was first developed into a practical device in the model yacht racing classes early in the Thirties. In 1936, the French translantic yachtsman Marin Marie evolved and made up a workable full-sized vane gear while crossing the Atlantic from West to East in the 45ft Motor Cruiser *Arielle*, but it was not until 1955 that effective vane gears appeared on full sized sailing boats: Ian Major's *Buttercup*, and Michael Henderson's *Mick the Miller*.

Since then, the Observer Trophy Singlehanded Translantic Races of 1960 and 1964 have given a great boost to vane gear development, and they are now becoming commonplace in most British yachting centres.

(2) H. G. (Blondie) Hasler, the originator of the singlehanded Translantic Race, first started developing vane gears on sailing models in 1953, and has remained the leader in the field ever since, gaining practical experience from four singlehanded crossings of the North Atlantic in his radical 25ft. Chinese-rigged *Jester*. Each of these crossings is believed to have set up a new record for boats of less than 30ft. overall, culminating in a passage of $33\frac{1}{2}$ days from Newport R.I. to the Solent, in July 1964. Out of a total of 12,000 miles *Jester* was steered by hand for less than 50 miles.

(3) The value of these steering gears on long voyages is obvious, but many owners of vane gears have no intention of crossing oceans,

Hasler pendulum-servo gear

and use their gears when cruising to save having to call on unwanted crew members. A good vane gear will steer the yacht on all points of sailing whenever there is a wind, and can be regarded as the equivalent of at least one, if not two extra men.

What are the Limiting Conditions?

(4) Hasler vane gears have steered yachts successfully in winds too light to be detectable to a person standing on deck.

At the end of the scale, they have coped with full gale conditions, including running on bare poles. It is not considered necessary to unship any part of the gear in severe weather, even when hove-to.

(5) Under any conditions where the yacht is difficult to steer by hand, she will also be difficult to steer by vane gear, but most difficulties can be resolved by reducing sail area when she gets wild on the helm.

Are they safe?

(6) It is still occasionally suggested that Vane Steering Gears are in some way "dangerous." This is nonsense.

We do not recommend that yachts should sail blindly around with nobody on watch.

Vane steering gears enable a solitary watchkeeper to keep a better look-out (for example, he can move position from which he can see under the genoa, or can stand up and use binoculars), and he can frequently visit the chart table when piloting through coastal waters.

All Hasler gears may be thrown out of action by pulling the latch line leading to the cockpit, enabling the watchkeeper to revert instantly to manual steering in an emergency.

Can I fit one to my Boat?

(7) Over the past four years Hasler Vane Gears have been fitted to over 40 yachts, ranging in size from 12ft. to 46ft. overall. Seven of these took part in the 1964 singlehanded Translantic race, and all reported satisfactory steering on all points of sailing and in all wind strengths.

(8) M.S. Gibb Ltd. has now acquired the sole licence of manufacure, and selling of these gears, and will produce them in two standardized types. It is claimed that one type or the other will be suitable for any sailing boat of between four and eighteen tons. Yachts above or below these limits can usually be fitted by special arrangement.

How much of the job does Gibb undertake?

(9) M. S. Gibb Ltd. will supply all the specialized hardware for the standard types of gear, and a few timber components, together with instructions for making up the remaining timber items, and installing the gear. Yacht owners who are reasonable amateur carpenters can do all this work themselves, but most owners employ a yard or yacht builder to do it for them.

Can I get individual advice on my installation?

(10) The aim is to supply instructions that will enable the owner or his chosen yacht yard to order, install and use the gear without individual consultation. For those owners however who prefer to get expert personal advice, H. G. Hasler and his associates will quote directly for their design and advisory services, on request.

(H. G. Hasler, The Old Forge, Curdridge, nr. Southampton, Hampshire. Tel.: Botley 2918).

What are the standard types of Vane Gear and how do they work?

(11) There are two types: Trim-Tab gears, and Pendulum-Servo gears. Both work on the servo principle, in which a small wind-vane is used to turn an underwater servo blade, whereupon the force of the water acting on the servo blade develops the power to turn the yacht's main rudder, which is left free.

The choice of which type of gear to order is determined by the type of rudder (as will be explained), and NOT by the owner's preference.

Trim-Tab Gears

(12) These must be ordered for all boats with externally-mounted rudders, i.e. with transom or lifeboat sterns.

In this well-known system, (Fig. 1) the wind vane V turns the Trim tab T, and the flow of water past the tab causes the rudder R to swing in the opposite direction. Hasler Trim-Tab gears incorporate a differential action to prevent oversteering, and can be shipped, or unshipped with the boat afloat, even at sea in reasonably calm weather.

The Tab shaft is protected by a tube trunk, P, which unships with it, and whose lower end carries the intermediate bearing. An average Trim-Tab gear complete with vane assembly, and latch gear will weigh about 35 lbs.

Pendulum-Servo Gears

(13) This new system has been invented by H. G. Hasler specifically to meet the demand for a fully portable vane gear that can be fitted to yachts with internal rudder stocks, without underwater modification. This type of gear must be ordered for all boats whose rudder stocks are internal, i.e. pass up through the Hull inside a rudder trunk.

(14) In this system, a servo blade S (Fig. 2) is hung vertically over the stern, and is carried by a servo box F which allows it to be turned like a rudder by means of the servo tiller A. The servo frame itself is carried in fore-and-aft Bearings E on the portable tubular bumpkin B, and can swing from side to side like an athwartships pendulum, taking the servo blade with it.

(15) A quadrant P (Fig. 2) is integral with the servo box, and steering ropes W lead from it through the sheaves C to the quadrant Q which is integral with the rudder stock. The wind vane V turns the servo tiller A, which turns the servo blade S. The flow of water past the bottom of the blade causes this and the servo box F to swing sideways (D), so that the quadrant P pulls the ropes W and so turns the Quadrant Q and the rudder R. Note: Fig. 2 is purely diagrammatic, and does not show the true proportions or layout of the components.

(16) When racing, all components of a pendulum servo gear may be stowed away in the foc'sle, ready for any subsequent cruising or day sailing. They may be shipped or unshipped at sea even in heavy weather. A type I.F.Q.H. pendulum gear, complete with its bumpkin and vane assembly weighs about 65 lbs.

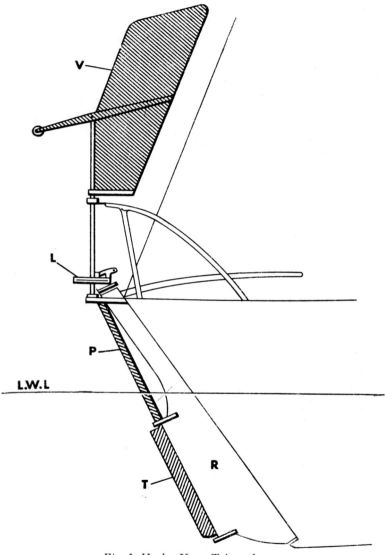

Fig. 1 *Hasler Vane Trim-tab gear*

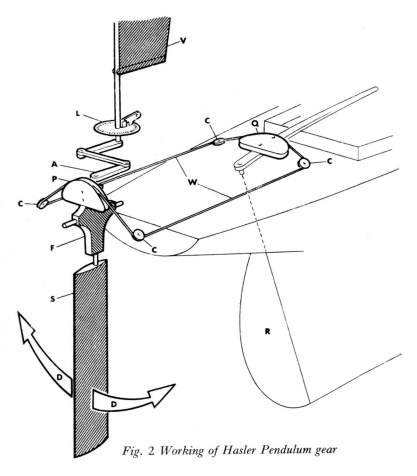

Fig. 2 Working of Hasler Pendulum gear

How are they controlled and set?

(17)   All Hasler gears use his standard vane, shaft and latch gear. This is normally mounted at least 8 in. to port or starboard of the centreline, and supported by an upper bearing carried on a bracket from the top rail of the aft pulpit, or by a special stanchion. The latch L selects the course to be steered relative to the apparent wind, and is worked by a line leading forward to a point within easy reach of the helmsman, so that the gear can be instantly disconnected in case of an emergency. The latch line also enables the watchkeeper to reset course without going far.

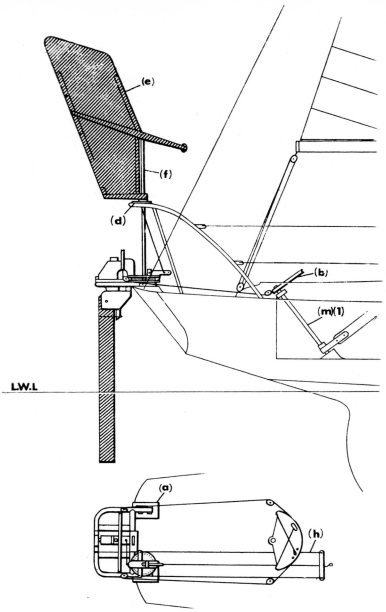

LW.L

Fig. 3 Hasler Pendulum gear

79

(18)   A further refinement in control is the "Brownstick" (based on an original experiment by Neville Brown, Esq., in *AMADIA*) which enables the watchkeeper, (using one hand only, and sitting in the cockpit) to unlatch the gear, steer the yacht by turning the servo blade manually, and latch up again, all in one series of movements.

What about the Shape of the Wind Vane?

(19)   A wide selection of shapes for the plywood vane usually enable it to be made so as to swing clear through 360 deg. of any obstruction.   Scale drawings of the standard wind vane will be supplied with the gear.

TRIM TAB GEARS

What is involved in installing a Trim Tab Gear?

(20)   Fig. 4 shows to scale, a typical trim tab gear (type T.E.B.-8) installed on a transom sterned six tonner.   Before ordering such a gear it is necessary to obtain from M. S. Gibb Ltd. the pamphlet, "How to Order a Trim Tab type of Vane Gear," which gives instructions for determining certain variables.

(21)   Your vane gear components will then be delivered with detailed instructions for the work of installation which may be summarised as follows:

(Small letters in Fig. 4 refer to these sub-paragraphs)

(a) Determine by trial the exact alignment of the axis of the main rudder hangings in relation to the rudder head.

Hasler trim-tab on yacht KLOMPEN (Rudder on right)

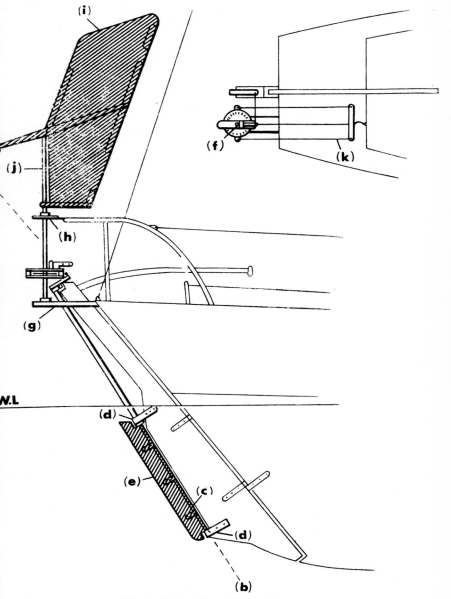

Fig. 4 Hasler Vane Trim-tab gear

81

(b) Remove main rudder, use a template or the actual components and lay out the exact line of the tabshaft on it, and the position of the tabshaft gudgeons.

(c) Produce the necessary length of straight trailing edge on the rudder, commonly by planing off some of the round, and gluing a small pad at either end of this length. Modify the rudder head as necessary to carry the head of the Tabshaft trunk.

(d) Fit the two Tabshaft gudgeon fittings permanently to the rudder.

(e) Make up the timber trim-tab, and fit it to the tabshaft straps.

(f) Replace the main rudder on the yacht. Ship the tabshaft assembly, and crosslink, and hence position the vane shaft and latch gear, (commonly at least 10in. to port or starboard of the centre line).

(g) Provide a platform (commonly a stub bumpkin) to carry the lower vane shaft bearing.

(h) Provide a metal bracket, about 2 ft. above deck level, to carry the upper vane shaft bearing. This bracket may be bolted or welded to the after pulpit, or may be carried by a separate stanchion of its own.

(i) Make the plywood wind vane, to our scale drawings.

(j) Cut and drill the tubular vane shaft to suit the vane and fit its "jumping collar."

(k) Lay out the control lines and position the brownstick, to suit the helmsman's position.

Possible complications are:

(l) Existing bumpkin, or bumpkin stays, may foul tabshaft trunk when rudder is hard over. Remedy: Alter bumpkin and/or stays to clear trunk.

(m) Boom end, and/or standing backstay, or foremost sheet may be too far aft to permit the vane shaft to be mounted in standard position. Remedy: Mount vane shaft further aft, if necessary on it's own "Gate bumpkin," and use the additional bell-crank linkage between vane shaft and cross-link.

(n) Wheel steering: provision must be made for disconnecting wheel steering gear from the rudder head whenever the vane gear is in use. An emergency tiller should always be shipped before this is done.

(o) If the yacht carries strong weather helm, heavy shock cord may be used to take some of the load off the tab gear.

What does a Trim-Tab cost?

(22) For boats of between 5 and 18 tons about £118 (Ex. Works carriage and packing extra) for the supply of the standard

specialized hardware, together with the standard instructions and drawings. Please note that this does not include individual design work, which is normally unnecessary. This can of course be provided separately (see para. 10).

It will then be necessary for the owner to make his own arrangements for fitting the gear supplied.

PENDULUM-SERVO GEARS

What is involved in installing a Pendulum Servo Gear?

(23) (Type I.F.Q.H.). Before ordering such a gear, it is necessary to obtain from M. S. Gibb Ltd., the pamphlet, "How to Order a Hasler Vane Gear (Pendulum Servo Type)" which gives instructions for determining certain variables.

(24) Your vane gear will then be delivered complete with detailed instructions for the work of installation, which can be done with the boat afloat and may be summarised as follows:

(a) Offer up the bumpkin base plates to the yacht, drill them for fastening, hot dip galvanize, and fit them permanently to the yacht.

(b) Make up and fit the plywood quadrant to the yacht's rudder head, with necessary brackets or flange.

(c) Ship the hinged bumpkin. Lay out the steering ropes, and fit the forward steering sheaves.

(d) Provide a metal bracket, about 2 ft above deck level to carry the upper vane shaft bearing. This bracket may be bolted or welded to the after pulpit, or carried by a separate stanchion of its own.

(e) Make up the plywood wind vane, to our scale drawings.

(f) Cut and drill the tubular vane shaft to suit the vane and fit to its "jumping collar."

(g) Provide a portable stop to limit main rudder movement to + or − 30 degrees when steering ropes are connected.

(h) Lay out control lines and position the brownstick, to suit the helmsman's position.

Possible complications are:

(i) Existing after pulpit may have a centre stanchion, or lower rail, that interferes with the shipping and unshipping of the servo assembly. Remedy: Modify the pulpit to remove the parts that foul.

(j) Existing centreline backstay may interfere with shipping and unshipping the servo assembly. Remedy: Either move its lower end further forward, or fit quarter plates and span the backstay to them (or fit twin backstays).

(k) Existing bumpkin (for backstay or mizzen sheet) and/or its stays may prevent fitting the standard pendulum servo bumpkin. Remedy: Either modify it to clear the standard servo bumpkin, or design a special bumpkin which does both jobs.

(l) Existing fittings such as stern light, ensign socket, or fairleads, (if within $13\frac{1}{2}$ in. of centreline) may get in the way of the gear. Remedy: Move them farther outboard.

(m) Top of yacht's rudder stock may be below deck level, e.g. just above the cockpit sole.
Remedy:
(i) Fit extension (permanent or portable) to the rudder stock to bring it above deck level, or
(ii) Fit a purchase or lever to each steering rope to increase its travel, then lead the ropes direct to the tiller, at 20 in or 30 in. radius.
(iii) Use additional sheaves to lead the steering ropes down to a quadrant below deck level.

(n) Boom end, or aftermost sheet, may interfere with swing of vane.
Remedy:
(i) Fit alternative type I.A.Q.H. gear, which carries the vane 23 in. further aft, on a variation of the standard bumpkin, and/or
(ii) In a ketch or yawl, move the mizzen sheet forward along its boom, raise the boom if necessary, and swing a broad low vane underneath it, or
(iii) In a yawl, hand the mizzen if and when it is interfering with the vane, and stow it horizontally on top of the pulpit rail, so that the vane can swing over it. (A mizzen staysail may still be carried, providing it can be sheeted to the quarter or to the pulpit.)

(o) With wheel steering, do not try to swing the wheel by turning a quadrant on the rudder stock even if the gear is easily reversible. Instead you may
(i) Disconnect the wheel gear from the rudder stock when on vane steering, (e.g. by withdrawing a latch key or pin, or by disconnecting one end of the steering wire, or by a reliable form of dog clutch). An emergency tiller should always be shipped before this is done, or
(ii) Step up the rope travel, as in (m) (ii) above and use these augmented steering ropes to turn a small drum fitted to the boss of your steering wheel. In the standard design (which is based on an original experiment by Col. Odling-Smee in *NANISE*) the drum incorporates a friction clutch, and can be instantly released or readjusted by means of a large knurled nut.

(p) If the yacht sometimes carries a strong weather helm, heavy shock cord may be used to take some of the load off the servo gear.

What does it cost to fit a Pendulum-Servo Gear?

(25) For boats of between 5 and 18 tons, about £200 (ex Works carriage and packing extra) for the supply of the standard specialized hardware (type I.F.Q.H.) together with instructions and drawings. Type I.A.Q.H. cost about £10 more.

It will be necessary for the owner to arrange for the fitting of the gear, and it should be noted that the price does not include individual design work which is normally unnecessary but this can be provided (see para. 10).

(26) If you have studied all the information given here, and wish to proceed further, please ask M. S. Gibb Ltd., Warsash, to supply one of the more detailed pamphlets which is applicable to your boat. Either

"HOW TO ORDER A TRIM-TAB TYPE OF VANE GEAR"
or
"HOW TO ORDER A PENDULUM-SERVO TYPE OF VANE GEAR"

THE " QUARTERMASTER " GEAR
BY H. K. WILKES
Firlawn, Dene Close, Chilworth, Southampton.

When I designed the " Quartermaster " self-steering gear for my *FOLKBOAT*, I set out to produce one which would be efficient, but which would not require any modifications to the yacht, which could be easily removed for racing, and could readily be fitted again, either at moorings or even under way, when required.

Initial trials in 1965, using various " feed-back " linkages, though theoretically sound, were disappointing. Eventually, I finished up with a very simple arrangement which works most satisfactorily in all conditions, is easy to fix and operate, and is relatively inexpensive. The gear works on the trim-tab principle, the wind vane being directly linked to the trim-tab. Turning the trim-tab causes the water flow to exert a lateral pressure on the tab, which, being directly mounted on the rudder stock, moves the rudder. Setting the wind vane to the wind for the course required, or alteration of course or tack is made by operating from the cockpit a light lanyard attached to a latch engaging notches in a dial on the wind vane staff. The secret of holding a steady course on any point of sailing is the use of light shock cord on

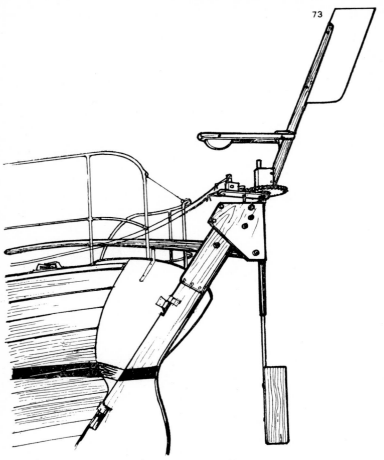

The " Quatermaster " gear

the tiller, and (in a following wind) in using loose tiller lines to limit the swing of the tiller. Practice is required to obtain optimum results.

The gear steers a remarkable windward course. Trials in 1965 with recording instruments showed that the " Quartermaster " brought the yacht better to windward than I could, steering manually. The graphs of these tests are shown earlier in this book, on page 8. On the 1966 Round the Isle of Wight Race, we set the " Quartermaster " and crossed the starting line exactly ten minutes behind the main fleet of over 300 yachts. The first 13 miles to the Needles was a long-and-short tack beat in force 3-4. Except to tack, neither the gear nor tiller was touched. At the Needles buoy, we hove-to and counted 22 boats, including six *FOLKBOATS*, rounding behind us. On several occasions, we had had to bear away to give room to a yacht sagging down to leeward and it was clear that the " Quartermaster " scored by pointing up better and sailing at a smaller angle of heel.

Any efficient gear shows to best advantage when sailing on the wind. With the wind aft, some yawing must be expected since the gear reacts to the apparent wind. Few realise how much a change in the speed of the true wind, even when constant in direction, alters the direction of the apparent wind. Yawing so caused may be appreciable in sheltered waters but is seldom a problem in the open sea.

Anyone who has used one will agree that an efficient gear, even for day sailing, adds greatly to the pleasure, and the benefits are still more marked when passage-making. Single-handed or short-handed cruising is infinitely easier and sail changing, including setting a spinnaker, presents no problems. We shall see many more boats with self steering as time goes by.

The " Quartermaster " gear is manufactured by Bingley, Son & Follit Ltd., Minerva Road, London, N.W.10.

PEN DUICK II's GEAR

The M.N.O.P. " Gymnop " mechanism used by Eric Tabarly on *PEN DUICK II* is an interesting and sophisticated gear. It consists of a horizontally pivoted vane which can be rotated on a vertical axis by remote control to set the course to be self steered. Movement of the vane on its horizontal axis (it is in fact mounted 10° out of horizontal) actuates a separate rudder hung over the counter of *PEN DUICK II*. The movement of the vane causes a push rod to be moved up or down. This vertical movement of the push rod is converted into rotary movement of the rudder by a cam track on the rudder spindle—a similar action to the " Yankee " pump screwdrive where vertical movement of the handle causes the screwdriver blade to rotate.

Adjustment of the Vane Angle. The vane bearings which give the horizontal rotation are, in turn mounted on a vertically pivoted drum which moves freely but can be clamped by a cord running in a groove on the drum's perimeter and led through blocks to the deck, from where it can be controlled by a separate line. When the tension on the cord is released, the drum is free to rotate and the vane will swing into line with the wind. When the drum is clamped, any change in wind direction will cause the vane to swing on its horizontal axis and actuate the rudder.

Adjustment of the Mechanical Advantage of the Vane. The push rod attached to the vane carries at its lower end a horizontal bar, one end of which engages the cam track on the rudder spindle. The other end of this bar moves in a slot which takes the torque reaction of the cam track. If the slot is parallel to the cam track, then vertical movement of the push rod and the bar will not cause any rudder rotation, the lower end of the push rod swinging sideways as it moves. If, however, the slot is rotated until it is vertical, then movement of the push rod will cause the bar to twist and the rudder to rotate. The mechanical advantage can therefore be adjusted by varying the angle of the slot.

The " Gymnop " Mechanism. This is an air turbine driven gyroscope mounted on the vane drum at right angles to the vane, and it rotates with the vane when the course to be sailed is adjusted.

The turbine, being at right angles to the windflow, rotates and the heavy perimeter of the turbine acts as a gyroscope. Should the boat lurch off course, the gyroscope will continue to point in the correct direction. The gyroscope is pivoted on a vertical spindle and any deviation from the course set will result in the gyroscope moving a " servo tab " on the trailing edge of the vane. The vane will then be

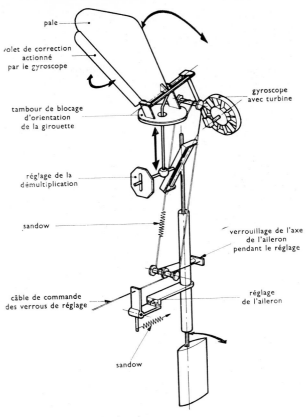

pale

/olet de correction
actionné
par le gyroscope

tambour de blocage
d'orientation
de la girouette

gyroscope
avec turbine

réglage de la
démultiplication

sandow

verrouillage de l'axe
de l'aileron
pendant le réglage

câble de commande
des verrous de réglage

réglage
de l'aileron

sandow

16. *Ensemble de la gi-
rouette M.N.O.P.*

PEN DUICK'S gear

acted upon by the wind and, swinging on its horizontal spindle, will apply correcting rudder action.

This self steering mechanism integrates two separate factors. The vane on its own would be a good self steering gear as shown by the Gunning gear of a later article. The gyroscope, too, on its own should also be able to self steer, using the vane as an air-driven pendulum, as opposed to the water-driven pendulums. It is not known why it was felt necessary to have both of these on the one gear.

A Gyroscope's " Precession." " Precession " is the feature of a gyroscope which causes it to twist in an axis at 90° to the axis at which outside twisting is applied. It will have been seen by everyone in tops as they slow down, when they begin to wobble. With the Gymnop gear on *PEN DUICK* with a beam wind, a sudden roll to leeward would therefore apply bias to the servo on the vane and therefore on the rudder. Because the direction of rotation of the gyroscope was always the same, this would only be correct for one tack with extra weather helm. On the opposite tack, lee helm would be supplied, with a sudden roll to leeward.

THE GYROSCOPIC GEAR

It is not known how well the Gymnop gear worked on *PEN DUICK II*. Nor is it known how much wind is needed to make the gyroscope spin or if the " Air-pendulum " system was better than a

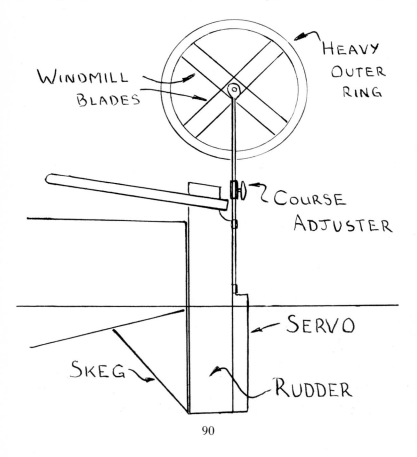

water pendulum. A good deal of experiment would therefore be needed to make a gyroscopic gear workable. The effects of " precession " might indeed make the gear impossible, though it should be possible to overcome this.

It is, however, most important to investigate the gyroscopic gear for multihulls surfing in strong winds. One of the gears already described will most certainly steer any boat in light winds, down to force 1 and we should at least endeavour to cover all conditions of sailing.

The simplest way to use the gyroscope is to mount it instead of the vane on a " Moving carriage " gear and take the downshaft to a balanced rudder, pendulum or trim-tab. Instantaneous disengagement in the downshaft would be the method of choice, we think.

The *PEN DUICK* gear tried, we think, to combine two different systems and the result was far too great a sophistication to be seaworthy. Surely, it would be better to have some sort of moving carriage gear with a horizontal pivoted vane for light winds. Some sort of provision should then be made to replace the vane by the gyroscope for strong following winds. Alternatively, two quite separate gears could be carried, one of each sort which would be the utterly seamanlike thing to do.

THE *PEN DUICK* GEAR AND THE GUNNING MODIFICATION

BY M. F. GUNNING, M.R.I.N.A.

Little Hawsted, Steep, Petersfield, Hants, England.

(Condensed from an article for *Yachting Monthly* by kind permission of the Editor)

The great majority of vane gears are of the simple windvane type i.e., they swing round a vertical shaft. Tabarly, however, in *PEN DUICK II*, used a vane swinging round a horizontal axis, for which he claims, in my opinion rightly, great advantages.

There are four factors which may cause trouble with all vane gears. These are : 1. Friction. 2. Inertia. 3. The apparent wind and 4. The windspeed.

1. As regards friction, one must remember that, roller bearing excepted, friction at rest may be as much as ten times greater than the friction once motion has started. So, in light winds, a considerable angle of incidence of wind on the vane may be required before the vane starts to move and once started, it is apt to rush off, like a slow-witted helmsman.

91

2. Inertia has much the same effect as friction. A gear with a great built-in inertia will be slow to start, and once started, slow to stop. However, on occasion inertia may be beneficial.

3. The effect of the apparent wind is more complicated but it may be summarised by saying that, for a close-hauled yacht, a change in direction of the true wind is always very much greater than the change in direction of the apparent wind. Therefore fine control of the vane setting should be available if wanted.

4. As regards wind speed, say a gear works satisfactorily with a wind of 10 knots, the yacht doing 5 knots. Now increase the wind to 20 knots when the yacht may be doing 7 knots. In general, forces vary roughly with the square of the speed so the force on the rudder is doubled while that on the vane is quadrupled. It is surprising that most gears seem to be able to cope with this difference, but some means of roughly adapting vane size to the force of the wind seems desirable.

Now consider the working of the usual vane, with vertical shaft. Suppose the wind veers 10°, and so will strike the vane at that angle, forcing it over. By the time it has moved 5°, the angle of incidence, and with it the force on the vane will be halved. It is obvious either that the vane must be very large, or the gear will be slow to respond.

As regards the setting of the vane, we have seen that this must be done to very fine limits. Some gears do this by means of friction clutches which are apt to slip, and difficult to operate from a distance. So most gears have a gearwheel fitted to the vane, and a little tumbler to the trim-tab or other shaft, which can lock the vane to the shaft and be lifted by means of a line led to within easy reach of the helmsman. The yacht is brought on course with a little bias as indicated by practice, and the vane will set itself to the wind. Then the tumbler is released and it engages with one of the teeth of the gearwheel, thus locking the vane in the desired position.

It all sounds delightfully simple, but the snag lies in the fact that these gearwheels usually do not seem to have more teeth than 36 (more would make the wheel too large or the teeth too small), and that means setting to within 10° only and that is not good enough.

The action of the *PEN DUICK* vane is somewhat difficult to understand. Imagine the vane, and the horizontal axis round which it pivots, heading directly into the wind. When the wind veers, it will strike one side of the vane, forcing it over. But in doing so, the vane will *not* lose the wind, at least not during the relatively small angles we are dealing with. It acts like a windmill, with the sails set at a very small angle. It will go over, taking the trim-tab " Pendulum " or tiller of a balanced rudder with it, until the latter really bites, and begins to bring the ship back on the desired course. The vane, with its long leading edge and high aspect ratio is sensitive to wind striking it at small angles, and thus it is quick to react, like a keen helmsman.

The *PEN DUICK* vane has other advantages. It will easily clear the backstay. It can be fitted halfway between the bearings on which it pivots, thus reducing friction to a minimum. It can easily be removed altogether, so that two vanes may be carried, for light and heavy weather. Being more effective, it can be smaller and lighter with smaller counterweights and greatly reduced inertia. A final great advantage is that it is set at a fixed bearing relative to the *Ship*, as opposed to the ordinary vane, which is set relative to the trim-tab, "Pendulum" or auxiliary rudder. This makes continuous and remote control a far easier proposition. I have no doubt that the *PEN DUICK* vane is much better than the other type.

Existing gears of other types

1. The Directly Acting Vane. When the vane works directly on the rudder, as in Chichester's *MIRANDA*, the vane has to be large and, I think it is rather impractical. But I have seen it work perfectly on a little *JOG* type 20 footer. The gear developed by Michael Henderson for the Prout catamaran *RANGER* is also of this type but is said to be inoperative below wind force 3.

2. The Auxiliary Rudder. A vane can work a small auxiliary rudder of about one quarter of the size of the main one. This reduces the size of the vane and gear in proportion. It may be asked why a small rudder will do the job. Does this mean that the main rudder is hopelessly over size? In fact, the main rudder has to do many things which will not be required of the auxiliary one, notably bringing the yacht about. The main advantage of the auxiliary rudder is that it is small, so that violent movements of the vane will not greatly affect the ship, thus reducing oversteer.

3. Tab Gears. The area of the tab will be perhaps one fifth of that of the main rudder. Now the tab exerts a force opposite to that of the rudder and this force is willy nilly transmitted to the ship, giving it a wrong turning moment equal to $\frac{1}{4}$ of that exercised by the main rudder. About $\frac{1}{4}$ of the main rudder must be used to compensate this, leaving it only $\frac{3}{4}$ effective. The answer is to move the tab away from the rudder stock, increasing its leverage and so reducing its size. The "Tubernet" gear (see the article by Gianoli) does this in a simple and elegant way.

4. The Hasler Pendulum Gears. With these, the first feature that claims our attention is that the pendulum doubles, in a small way ,

as an auxiliary rudder. That is, it does not oppose the action of the main rudder, but assists it. This, of course, is simply a matter of the manner in which the vane is linked to the tab, and the pendulum linked to the rudder.

The Hasler pendulum gear has been used with great success on a variety of yachts. Nevertheless, it appears to be open to two objections. First of all, an ordinary vane is used, with all the disadvantages this entails. Secondly, the support of the auxiliary rudder is open to criticism. It cantilevers out over 5 feet or more, supported by two closely spaced bearings. This results in large bearing loads, friction and bending moments in the blade.

So we see that many types of gears are available, and most seem to operate well, remarkably so in view of the wide variety of conditions they have to cope with. However, successful operation does not mean that no improvements are required, otherwise we would all still be driving a Ford " T " or its sisters.

Two years ago, I designed a gear (ordinary vane-cum-tab) for a hard-mouthed 13 tonner. The owner sent back enthusiastic reports, averaging 127 miles a day over 18 days running down the Trades. But later he asked me to provide continuous remote control for the vane, and to eliminate the cause of oversteer, rather than cure it with shock-cord and what-not.

So when this year a gear was designed for a sister ship, I took a completely fresh look at things, found and patented a simple way to transmit the movement of the *PEN DUICK* vane to the tab, and improved the pendulum gear by splitting the blade into a fixed skeg and a rear part which can be turned, the two forming an aerofoil section. This enabled me to place the blade between two lightly loaded bearings fixed to the skeg, and to attach stays to the skeg, supporting it at waterline level. The stays double as tiller lines and are led over ordinary spreaders, giving great leverage, with corresponding reduction in forces in the tiller lines.

The connection of the vane to pendulum consists of two thin wires led over a quadrant on the vane over sheaves and down the centre of the " mast "—a 1½ inch tube, on which the vane is fitted. At the bottom of the " mast " these wires pass over further sheaves to the quadrant on the stock of the steering part of the pendulum. When the fitting which supports the vane is turned to set the course, the wires are twisted but, as the movement is restricted to 180° each way, this does not matter. The vane mounting is fitted with a grooved flange, round which a wire is wound. By pulling one end or the other of this line, the vane can be turned and set to fine limits, if needs be from the doghouse.

VANE SET FOR BEAM WIND

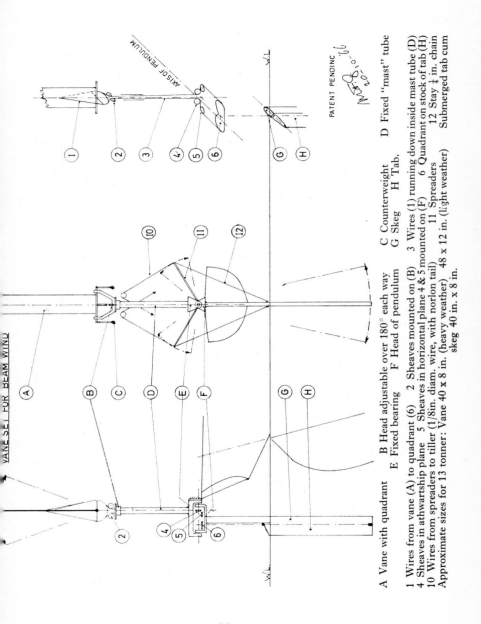

PATENT PENDING

A Vane with quadrant   B Head adjustable over 180° each way   C Counterweight   D Fixed "mast" tube
     E Fixed bearing   F Head of pendulum   G Skeg   H Tab.

1 Wires from vane (A) to quadrant (6)   2 Sheaves mounted on (B)   3 Wires (1) running down inside mast tube (D)
4 Sheaves in athwartship plane   5 Sheaves in horizontal plane 4 & 5 mounted on (F)   6 Quadrant on stock of tab (H)
10 Wires from spreaders to tiller (1/8in. diam. wire, with norlon tail)   11 Spreaders   12 Stay ¼ in. chain
Approximate sizes for 13 tonner: Vane 40 x 8 in. (heavy weather)   48 x 12 in. (light weather)   Submerged tab cum
     skeg 40 in. x 8 in.

95

A spring-loaded lock is fitted which keeps the vane amidships when not in use. When it is to be used, the ship is brought on course and the vane set to head into the wind. Then the lock is pulled out and the vane takes over, final correction being made by adjusting the vane-setting lines. In fact, the ship has been piloted through crowded waters without touching the helm, just by operating these lines.

The effectiveness of the vane, and the strength of the pendulum make it possible to make the gear much stronger than is required to operate the helm. The movement of the helm can then be limited by fitting a *Lee* tiller line, the pendulum carrying on as an auxiliary rudder, as described above. But the pendulum remains always free to put the helm alee, when required. Thus, the gear can be made to cope with a great variety of conditions by restricting or otherwise its freedom to operate the main rudder.

The gear has fully come up to expectations. Some commercial interest is being taken so that it may be possible to bring out a production model before long.

THE A.Y.R.S. GEARS

BY JOHN MORWOOD

In order to invent anything, one has to know *only* the *conditions which must be satisfied.* The invention then usually springs to mind though details may need some working over.

When Tom Herbert sent me the manuscript for the revised issue of this publication, he had seen all the conditions for the best possible self steering gear, and had gone most of the way to satisfying them in a device. He now has completed his invention and we describe it later.

However, when his gear was in the half-invented stage, I was so delighted that we were about to break the back of the problem that I not only wrote to Tom in enthusiastic terms but also wrote to Jock Burrough and David Mole, putting the problem to them. They both, within days, sent in the devices we now show. M. F. Gunning, on the other hand, as his article so clearly shows, had worked out the needs for himself. Indeed, this article states the arguments against the gears which are now being used so clearly that nothing more need be said by me here. The best possible self steering gear will have the following attributes :

1.   The vane will develop the greatest possible work on a windshift. This can only be produced by a vane with a horizontal or near horizontal axis.

96

2. Course-setting must be easy, continuous and " fine " as with the " Moving carriage " gear. This means that the boat can be steered by control of the self steering gear only, the yacht's tiller waving about freely.

3. The gear must be capable of instant disengagement and manual steering in case of failure.

4. The gear must be easily removed from the boat so that it can be kept below in storms.

THE BURROUGH GEAR

Jock Burrough sailed *TAO* in the Round Britain Race with a Henderson running line gear and was pleased with it except for :—

1. Its inability to function in light and sloppy conditions.

2. Its poor working close hauled when cross seas were heavy in comparison to the wind speed and

3. The temporary failure when the trimaran was surfing with the wind astern.

Jock's first suggestion was therefore merely to use the running line gear with the vane mounted on a horizontal axis, thus only complicating the Henderson gear by two blocks. The vane, its counterweight and bearings would be mounted on a vertical axle so that it could weathercock when not in use. In use, the vertical axle would be fixed, thus making the vane rotate about the horizontal axis.

This gear has the advantage of being almost the simplest in this book. Because the Henderson running line gear works, this will work even better. It can have a bigger vane for light winds and will, of course, develop more work.

Course setting is by the two lines to the lower drum, though this will involve crossing of the lines down from the vane drum and hence be limited to about 180° from dead astern. When the vane is set, the line is put in the jamb cleats on the tiller, and instant disengagement is got by slipping it out.

The second suggestion by Jock Burrough is a method of avoiding having the lines cross in the above gear. The lines coming down from the vane, now pass through blocks on arms fixed to the vertical axle and go to a drum which can rotate around it. Lines from the drum go to the tiller as before. Course setting is by a lower drum and when this drum is turned, the vane is turned but the upper drum is also turned so the line must be disengaged from the tiller when altering the setting.

Jock's final suggestion is for the more sophisticated modification shown in Fig. 3. Here, a simple linkage converts the vertical swing of the vane to a horizontal rotation about a vertical axis.

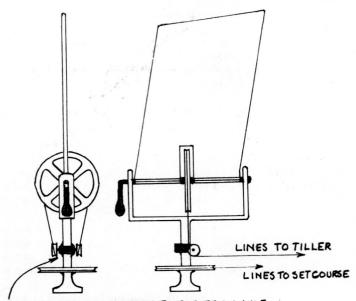

LINES TO TILLER

LINES TO SET COURSE

COLLAR WITH PULLEYS FREE TO ROTATE ON AXLE

Fig. 1   *Burrough gear Mark* 1

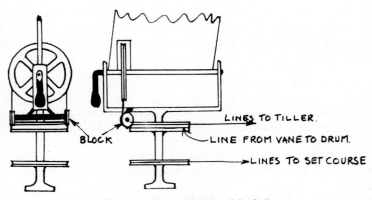

BLOCK

LINES TO TILLER.

LINE FROM VANE TO DRUM.

LINES TO SET COURSE

Fig. 2   *Burrough gear Mark* 2

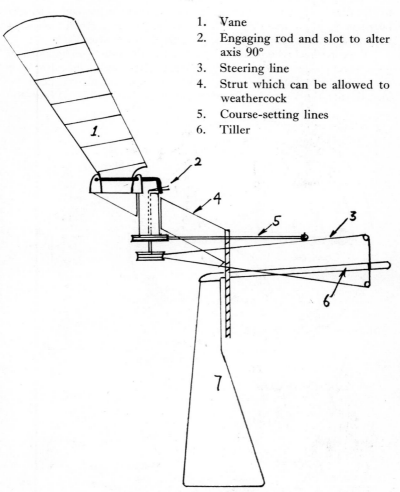

1. Vane
2. Engaging rod and slot to alter axis 90°
3. Steering line
4. Strut which can be allowed to weathercock
5. Course-setting lines
6. Tiller

Fig. 3 *Burrough gear Mark* 3

THE MOLE GEAR

Devised by DAVID MOLE, 115, Woodwarde Road, London, S.E.22.

This gear uses a vane to turn a drum from which lines go directly to the tiller. The vane-spindle is pivoted about a horizontal axis in bearings fixed to the drum. The drum, in turn, rotates about a vertical axis on a spindle in a bearing fixed to the after deck.

A gear-wheel (the " driver ") is fixed to the vane spindle and this gear wheel engages with a gear ring fixed to the deck concentric with the drum spindle. The vane, which is counterbalanced, can be locked onto the vane spindle by means of a " Clutch ". When the

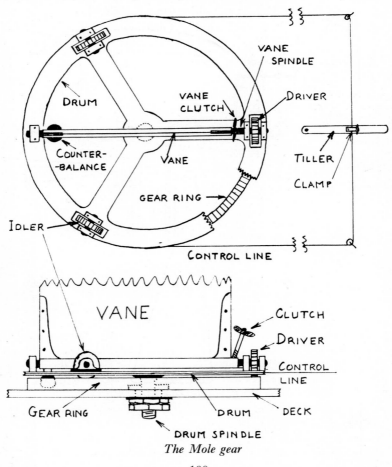

The Mole gear

clutch is disengaged, the vane is free to rotate about the spindle ; when it is engaged, rotation of the vane causes rotation of the " Driver " gear.

The drum carries a continuous line which passes through a clamp on the tiller. When the clamp is open and the vane clutch is disengaged, the drum can be rotated through 360° or more by moving the control line, there are two idler gears on the drum to ensure smooth rotation.

Operation. When the wind strikes one side of the vane, it tends to blow it flat. The subsequent rotation of the vane causes the driver gear to rotate. As the driver gear rotates on the gear ring, it forces the drum to rotate and thus moves the control line and hence the tiller.

Setting. To set the vane, the vane clutch is disengaged and the tiller clamp is opened. Then, with the boat on the desired course, the drum is rotated until the vane is aligned with the apparent wind. The control line is then clamped to the tiller and the vane clutch is engaged.

Comments. This gear has not been tried yet. The horizontally pivoted vane should give more power than a vertically pivoted one because the horizontally pivoted vane can move through 90° and does not reach zero angle of incidence until the ship is heading on the desired course, i.e., to any wind not aligned with the pivot. Operated as shown, with the driver gear upwind of the vane, rotation of the drum moves the vane further out of alignment with the wind, though only by a few degrees, and thus provides even more power.

THE MORWOOD GEAR

This is a modification of the *PEN DUICK* gear with the vertical push-pull rod acting on cranks to give a fore and aft movement which can actuate the rudder, trim-tab or pendulum. Continuous rotation is provided by having the push-pull fitted with a ball and socket joint at one end and mounting the vane bearings at one side of a drum whose central hole lets the push-pull rod pass through. In the drawing, it is shown revolving with friction, being held in place by long screws but a more friction-free system could be used.

Continuous and fine course-setting should be easy with this gear, while the vane gives ample power. Instantaneous disengagement is not shown. The simplest form would be to put it in the push rod at the bottom of the gear which goes to the rudder etc.

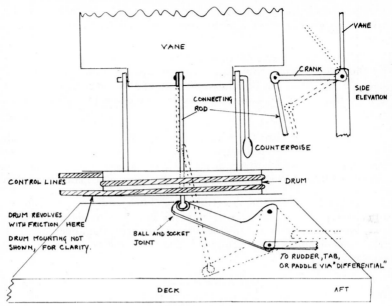

The Moorwood gear

THE HERBERT GEAR

The moving carriage vane mechanism has been used by Albert Wilcock with great success on model yachts. Its great merit is the ease and accuracy with which the vane angle can be adjusted. This mechanism seems to be well suited to full sized boats, particularly as it can be easily adapted to function with a horizontally pivoted vane, whose advantages have already been discussed.

The Herbert gear is in essence a combination of the moving carriage mechanism and the horizontally pivoted vane. The moving carriage enables the course setting to be precise and " fine " at any angle to the apparent wind, the carriage being remotely controlled by " tiller lines " around a drum on it. The boat can thus be steered manually with the vane in action by the " tiller lines " ; or the vane can be instantaneously disengaged by leaving the carriage free to rotate so that the vane movement is absorbed by the carriage.

The vane and carriage can be positioned clear of obstruction in " clear air " and the vane movement transmitted by a linkage to the rudder or servo-tab as required.

102

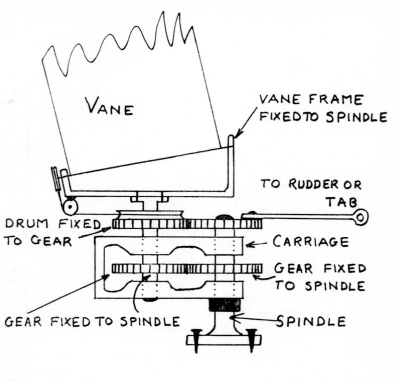

VANE

VANE FRAME FIXED TO SPINDLE

TO RUDDER OR TAB

DRUM FIXED TO GEAR

CARRIAGE

GEAR FIXED TO SPINDLE

GEAR FIXED TO SPINDLE

SPINDLE

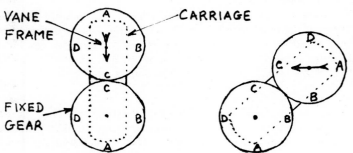

VANE FRAME

CARRIAGE

FIXED GEAR

DIAGRAM SHOWING HOW 45° ROTATION OF THE CARRIAGE GIVES 90° ROTATION OF THE VANE FRAME.

The Herbert gear

The mechanism is shown on Page 103 and works in the following manner :—

Vane movement is converted from rotation about the near-horizontal axis to rotation about a vertical axis by lines running from a pulley on the vane axle round sheaves to a drum attached to a gear wheel which can revolve freely on its axle. The gear wheel engages another of equal size also freely mounted on a spindle. A rod on the lower side of this gear wheel (not above as shown) can then steer the yacht through a balanced rudder, trim-tab, " paddle " or other way.

Both of the vertical axles are mounted in bearings and between them, they are supplied with gear wheels fixed to them which engage. Carriage movement, i.e., movement of the bearings of the vertical axles, taking the vane spindle with it, now causes the vane to twist about a vertical axis for course setting. A drum would be mounted around the carriage to which the " tiller lines " would be attached to give the course setting by remote control. Rotation of the carriage will then orientate the vane without disturbing it from a vertical position.

To self steer, the boat is steered by the mechanism onto the desired course by the " tiller lines " and they are then locked when the vane will continue the course set.

To ensure that the vane weather-cocks properly when the carriage is left free, the trailing edge of the vane should be well behind the pivoting point of the vane mounting, and the lines between the vane spindle pulley and the drum should be crossed. The crossed lines are not necessary if the vane spindle pulley is mounted at the higher leading end of the vane spindle.

The Herbert gear has not yet been tried out in practice and the proportions of the pulleys and drum from the vane spindle to the drum fixed to the gear wheel may be found to need alteration for any individual yacht. Tom Herbert is now making the gear and will be using it in the 1967 season. His address is as shown on the title page.

THE HYDRAULIC GEAR

This year (1967) we showed the self steering gear used by *DINAH* in the Round Britain Race—essentially a Hasler "pendulum gear"—at the Boat Show. We also had a model of Tom Herbert's gear made from Meccano. These created a good deal of interest and chatter about self steering in general. One visitor, whom I took to be a London doctor, though he wouldn't give his name said that he had been mulling over the problem from the hydraulic angle with a vane rotating around a horizontal axis and A. D. Ost wrote a letter to me

with further suggestions on the same theme. Once the matter has
been stated thus, the whole idea immediately falls into place as follows:

The Vane Mechanism. The vane is mounted on two bearings
so as to rotate about the horizontal axis. A side strut is connected to
the plunger of a hydraulic ram whose cylinder is mounted at the base
of the unit with some degree of freedom. The base of the unit is a
vertical axle with bearings so it can rotate freely and the hydraulic
pipe leads out through this.

The Tiller Mechanism. The hydraulic pipe leads to another
piston and cylinder mounted at the side of the cockpit, the piston
movement moving the tiller.

Advantages. The main advantage of the hydraulic system is the
fact that the vane mechanism can be mounted *Anywhere*—at the mast
head, the bow or either quarter. Continuous and fine course adjustment is, of course, possible and immediate disengagement is possible
through the use of a "by pass" valve, as is "sensitivity" to control
oversteer. One other and very valuable asset exists in the fact that
the whole gear can be taken below in storms, though one thinks that
this is the seamanlike procedure for any gear.

THE "AUTOMATE" WIND VANE STEERING GEAR

The "Automate" wind vane steering gear was designed several
years ago by J. R. Flewitt, A.M.R.I.N.A., to provide a cheap and portable
solution to the self steering problem in a small yacht of about 3 tons
displacement. Since installing the wind vane this yacht has cruised
extensively to such places as Biscay, Ireland and the Faroe Islands,
and the owner has written at great length of the usefulness of the gear
on both short and long passages.

He has kindly agreed to this gear being produced in quantity so
that for the first time it is available to all small boat owners. He has
also prepared very full instructions on how the best performances may
be obtained.

The whole of the self steering unit is carried by a standard outboard motor bracket as used for the British Seagull Century motors.
This has the advantage that the usual form of auxiliary power and the
vane gear are interchangeable and can both be stowed below when
not in use. The standard gear is made to fit the Seagull bracket which
is particularly neat. Special mountings can, however, be made at
small extra cost for other types of outboard motor bracket if full
details are provided.

The "Automate" gear

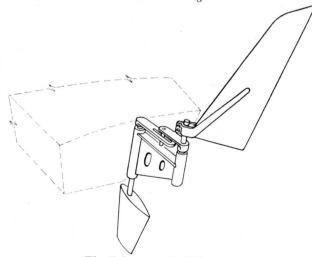

The "Automate" Fisher gear

The standard design is suitable for all small yachts of up to about 19ft. L.W.L., having the rudder *not* mounted on the transom. At some extra charge a larger version of the gear can be manufactured to individual customers requirements.

THE " KITE " RIGS

It is part of the A.Y.R.S. to conjecture *Every* conceivable method of interaction between wind and water (or, for that matter, wind and wind ; water and water) which will result in travel. One line of thought in this process is to draw a boat along either with a free flying kite or one in which the string is replaced by a light alloy pole which

Geoffrey Mile's Kite rig in his "Wind tunnel"

supports it in light winds. The ultimate in this line would be a " sail glider " flying in the air with the crew aboard and 100 to 200 feet of wire from it running down to a hydrofoil in the water. One of us (Morwood) has actually sailed to windward with a canvas wing at the end of a pole and the photograph shows a model application by Geoffrey Miles. The aerodynamics are a little hard to understand, especially with a free-flying kite but it is certainly a possible method of sailing. One of the bonuses of most kite rigs is the self steering which automatically appears.

Dear Sir,

The drawing may show one way of obviating the need for a "reefing vane" by reducing the lever arm for strong winds. An adjustable mass balance might be necessary.

I am rather frightened of "Pendulum gears". The thin blade mounted on the end of a counter needs to be very long to allow for pitching, which puts tremendous bending strains on it. How about

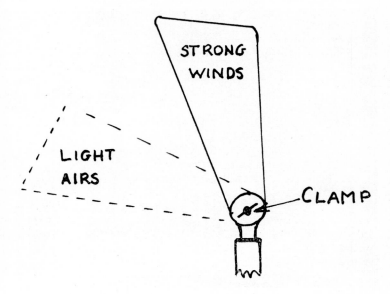

a throwback to the side rudder? It can be easily shipped and unshipped from the cockpit and is always deeply immersed. It could be mounted to port or starboard and the adjustment would be easily accessible.

I have also toyed with the idea of twin vanes, one on each quarter, which could be angled in opposition to each other to reduce the "blind spot", or even angled to slightly oppose each other to reduce their power in strong winds.

GEORGE DIBB.

1, Heywoods Close, Teignmouth, Devon.

Dear Mr. Herbert,

First of all let me apologise for the trouble you must be having trying to decipher my scrawl. At the moment I am 10 days out from the Canary Islands en route towards Barbados and under twin spinnakers in the North East Trade Winds. *Stardrift* is rolling a bit with the following seas, and I find it much easier to write than type.

The best self-steering device that anyone has been able to dream up for the present is definitely a twin tab on the trailing edge of the main rudder powered by a wind vane. To get smooth and efficient self-steering it is necessary to build in a differential in the linkage between the tab and vane. This differential is the reason why Haslar's and Major's self-steering was so efficient, and why David Lewis and Val Howells were having trouble in the Single Handed Trans-Atlantic Race. Attempts like Chichester's to turn the whole of the rudder by vanes, are behind the times.

You may remember that my trouble was that *Stardrift* has an internal rudder trunk. This made the linkage more difficult and more expensive, but we managed to slip a brass rod behind the rudder stock through the hollow rudder trunk and connected it by side linkages to the tab. An internal rudder trunk definitely faces more problems of design, and most certainly adds to the expense of fitting, but the fact remains that it can be overcome. We were even contemplating drilling a hole through the stock for our brass rod, but luckily found we had just enough room in the hollow trunk.

And now for the big question—how has it all worked out? As you can imagine, we had a few qualms, as this is, as far as we know, the first time that a wind vane with trim has ever been used on a yacht with an internal rudder trunk. All the work was carried out with great ingenuity and many helpful suggestions by Mashfords' Shipyard at Cremyll, Plymouth. But the point of all the thought and trouble is that *Stardrifts'* self-steering device has been a sensational success.

I left Plymouth at the end of May and arrived in Vigo, Spain, after 10 days, another 10 days to Las Palmas, and here I am after 10 days west north west of the Cape Verde Islands with 1000 miles just coming up on the log. On the voyage to date from 50°N. to 20°N. I have encountered all strengths of wind from all directions in all types of sea conditions, yet the only time that I have steered *Stardrift* is into and out of port. For every other inch of the way the wind vane has been in charge. What more can one ask than that? I am single handed, and with the vane doing so much of the work another person on board would only be in my way.

The only unusual thing that I found was that with quartering wind and seas under main and head sails, the yacht tends to yaw badly and make a course to windward of the one desired. I found the answer to be to drop the main and proceed under head sails alone, when the vane keeps her perfectly on course. With twin spinnakers too, I no longer yoke the after guys to the tiller but take them directly to the cockpit sheet winches and let the vane look after the rudder. This is a great boon for a single hander, for it is a terrific struggle adjusting the guys on the tiller when the spinnakers are full of wind. I think probably, with an efficient wind vane, twin spinnakers are redundant. However, I had had them fitted before the vane and, so am making use of them. But for an ocean crossing it would be one expense less that could go towards the cost of fitting the vane and tab.

On the wind, of course, or with the wind on or just abaft the beam, the vane is better than any human helmsman.

I hope these few observations are of interest to you and any A.Y.R.S. Members who are involved in the self-steering problem. If for any reason you should like to contact me, then a letter addressed to 91A, The Broadway, London, S.W.19 will be forwarded on to me wherever I happen to be.

Thank you once more for your previous help and advice, and the time you gave to my problems. I shall drop you an occasional postcard if I arrive anywhere interesting.

BILL HOWELL.

P.S.—I made Barbados in 24 days. I believe this a record for a single hander on the Trade Wind route, the previous fastest being John Goodwin in *Speedwell* in 1956—he took 26 days.

Dear John,

Comparison of the work of the Horizontally and Vertically pivoted Vanes

The work done by the vane is a function of Vane area X Arm of centre of pressure of vane from pivot X angular movement of Vane X angle of incidence. Assuming constant wind speed and similarly sized and shaped vanes—the Arm of the Horizontally pivoted Vane (H.P.V.) will be at least three times greater than the Vertically pivoted Vane (V.P.V.). There will thus be a factor of 3 in favour of the H.P.V.

If the initial deflection of the vessel from the desired course is say 10 degrees and the vessel's speed does not alter, then the angle of incidence of the vane to the apparent wind will be initially 10 degrees both on the H.P.V. and V.P.V. This incidence will go to zero with

10 degrees movement on the V.P.V. and 90 degrees movement on the H.P.V. There will thus be a factor of 9 in favour of the H.P.V.

Thus the H.P.V. does 27 times more work than the V.P.V. Alternatively a vane of 1/9th the area could be used.

If the initial deflection of the vessel from the desired course is 20 degrees the advantage in favour of the H.P.V. is halved, while an initial deflection of 5 degrees would double the advantage in favour of the H.P.V.

Variations in the angle of the pivot from the horizontal produce some interesting results. For example if this is sloped forward the vane will be unstable unless the movement of the apparent wind is greater than the angle of this slope forward. Sloping aft as shown in one of the illustrations of the Herbert Gear will reduce the effectiveness of the vane.

JOCK BURROUGH.

44, Bedford Gardens, London, W.8.

POSTSCRIPT

This little book has brought the knowledge of Self Steering up to 1966 but the development is rapid at present and new gears are coming out almost daily. As a result of this book, we look forward to some very interesting developments of gears which will have to fulfil the needs of yachtsmen, while being simple and seamanlike. Let us re-state the needs of a seamanlike vane gear:

1. Greatest possible work produced by the vane.

2. Easy, continuous and "fine" course-setting.

3. Instantaneous disengagement and manual steering in case of failure.

4. The capacity of complete removal below.

The A.Y.R.S. wishes pleasant sailing and safe passage making to all yachtsmen. If our efforts on behalf of SELF STEERING make your voyages happier ones, we will be well content.

List of A.Y.R.S. Publications

Some of the above publications are out of print at present. Please write for the current list to:

The Amateur Yacht Research Society,
Woodacres, Hythe, Kent, England.

Made and Printed in Great Britain by F. J. Parsons Ltd., London, Folkestone & Hastings.